Excellence
in
First-Year Writing
2018/2019

The English Department Writing Program
and
The Gayle Morris Sweetland Center for Writing

Edited by
Dana Nichols

ISBN 978-1-60785-545-3

Table of Contents
Excellence in First-Year Writing

Excellence in First-Year Writing

EDWP Writing Prize Chairs

J. W. Hammond

Adrienne Raw

EDWP Writing Prize Committee

Annette Beauchamp

Rachel Girty

Bryan Kim-Butler

Matthew Liberti

Ryan McCarty

Emily McLaughlin

Casey Otemuyiwa

Lauren Sirota

Katie Van Zanen

Sweetland Writing Prize Chair

Dana Nichols

Sweetland Writing Prize Committee

Angie Berkeley

Jimmy Brancho

Cat Cassel

Raymond McDaniel

Carol Tell

Sweetland Writing Prize Judges

Louis Cicciarelli

Lillian Li

Simone Sessolo

Naomi Silver

Administrative Support

Laura Schulyer

Aaron Valdez

Winners List

Feinberg Family Prize for Excellence in First-Year Writing

Hassan Bazzi, "Piece of War"
Nominated by R. Bruno, English 125

Rose-Carmel Goddard, "Surmounting the Struggle of Medical Waste"
Nominated by Cat Cassel, English 125

Kara Semanision, "Power and Pedagogy: An Open Letter on C.C. Little"
Nominated by Katherine Hummel, English 125

Kelley Prize for Excellence in First-Year Writing

Kate Glad, "Chuck Too Close"
Nominated by Duygu Ergun, CompLit 122: The Aesthetic Configurations of Life

Aditya Ravi, "Lunchtime Epiphanies"
Nominated by Genta Nishku, CompLit 122: Engaged Writing

Excellence in Multilingual Writing

Xuanwen Huang, "Toyota Camry in China and the US: Same Name,
    Different Cars" *Nominated by Scott Beal, Writing 120*

Zhiyao Zhang, "How Consuming Transgenic Food Would Affect Human
    Immune Systems?" *Nominated by Shuwen Li, Writing 120*

Excellence in the Practice of Writing

Michelle Karls, "How to Succeed in Writing 100 Without Really Trying
    (Disclaimer: You Should Actually Try)"
Nominated by Stephanie Moody, Writing 100

Anonymous, "Who I Am and Who I Want to Be Cannot Connect"
Nominated by Gina Brandolino, Writing 100

Nominees

Feinberg Family Prize nominees (Narrative argument)

Student	Instructor
Vivianne Assor	Marlin Jenkins
Hassan Bazzi	R. Bruno
Ethan Matt	Moira Saltzman
Natalie Chang	April Conway
Carmelita Perrien Naccarato	Cat Cassel
Theresa Pham	R. Bruno
Atticus Raasch	Kelly Wheeler
Zachary Stoloff	April Conway
Carina Tedesco	Jillian Myers
Nayla Zylberberg	April Conway

Feinberg Family Prize nominees (Analytic Argument)

Student	Instructor
Bri Buchanan	Esther Witte
Jane Burnett	April Conway
Katherine Colleran	Katherine Hummel
Kelsey Collins	Megan Behrend
Shiv Dave	Marlin Jenkins
Angela Gosselin	Marlin Jenkins
Olivia M. Hintz	Rachel Girty
Pierce Hourihane	Annette Beauchamp
Sophia Li	April Conway
Meghan Monaghan	Matthew Liberti
Ava Padgett	Matthew Liberti
Caroline Parkinson	April Conway
Kara Semanision	Katherine Hummel
Christopher Shaari	April Conway

Derek Shan	Katherine Hummel
Pearl Sun	Mason Jabbari
Ronit Tiwary	Marlin Jenkins
Madeline Vaitas	Annette Beauchamp
Julia Zak	Matthew Liberti
Holly Zhang	April Conway

Feinberg Family Prize nominees (Research-Based Argument)

Student	Instructor
Cloe Allen	R. Bruno
Chloe Carlson	Kelly Wheeler
Melaina Climer	April Conway
Gustavo D'Mello	R. Bruno
Andrew Diebold	Matthew Liberti
Rose-Carmel Goddard	Cat Cassel
Jiaheng He	R. Bruno
Elka Hutcheson	Rachel Cawkwell
Max Jones	April Conway
Britney Karcho	Matthew Liberti
Anastasia Klukowski	April Conway
Caroline Levine	Katherine Hummel
Michael Lyons	Michelle May-Curry
Elizabeth Manevich	Rachel Girty
Edwin Mui	Kelly Wheeler
Bashair Pasha	Matthew Liberti
Rohan Patel	April Conway
Rachel Pordy	R. Bruno
Sindy Sariev	April Conway
John Sepp	Katherine Hummel
Domenik Shehaj	Katherine Hummel
Jacqueline Sun	R. Bruno

Samantha Toomey	Rachel Girty
Luke Turo	Annette Beauchamp
Emily Wang	Marlin Jenkins
Mia Zapata	April Conway

Kelley Prize for Excellence in First-Year Writing nominees

Student	Instructor
Adrian Bahri	Ryan McCarty
Haley Beverlin	Genta Nishku
Nisha Bharat	Anna Mapp
Ellese Chapados	Netta Berlin
Ryan Espitia	Ali Shapiro
Sophia Fortunato	Sascha Crasnow
Kate Glad	Duygu Ergun
Claire Goods	Leslie Stainton
Abigail Haile	Christopher Matthews
Claire Hao	James Faulkner
Megan Harrison	Shelley Manis
Afra Kamal	Anna Mapp
Katharina Kretzler	Susan Rosegrant
Abby Mancuso	Ali Shapiro
Miranda McCarthy	Christopher Matthews
Nathalie O'Hernandez	Lynn Carpenter
Celestean	Scott Beal
Charles Pardales	Scott Beal
Nishika Patel	Shubha Sarode
Alison Prendergast	Leslie Stainton
Marlon Rajan	Christopher Matthews
Aditya Ravi	Genta Nishku
Brendan Schornack	Shubha Sarode

Sydney Sirota	Rachel Cawkwell
Jena Vallina	Sarah Messer
Shannon Zheng	Duygu Ergun
Jane Zhou	Rachel Cawkwell

Excellence in the Practice of Writing nominees

Student	Instructor
Sabrina Acosta	Gina Brandolino
Alana Burke	Lillian Li
Rui Dong	Jimmy Brancho
Michael Hurlburt	Lillian Li
Isis Joseph	Cat Cassel
Michelle Karls	Stephanie Moody
Isabella Menzel-Smith	Simone Sessolo
Isabella Palacios	Jimmy Brancho
Casey Roback	Simone Sessolo
Cooper Rood	Stephanie Moody
Jacob Shin	Cat Cassel

Excellence in Multilingual Writing nominees

Student	Instructor
Xuanwen Huang	Scott Beal
Jingyi Jia	Scott Beal
Rong Jin	Shuwen Li
Yuxin Lin	Natalia Knoblock
Manako Mukai	Natalia Knoblock
Jian Sun	Shuwen Li
Wenxuan Zhao	Scott Beal
Zhiyao Zhang	Shuwen Li

Introduction

This volume marks the ninth anniversary of a publication featuring prize-winning writing produced by students in first-year writing courses. The Sweetland Center for Writing initiated this series in order to make student writing more visible and valued within the University community. During the past nine years, hundreds of students in first-year writing courses have read essays composed by their slightly more advanced peers. Because the essays in each volume are available in PDF form on the Sweetland website, it's easy for instructors and students to download them for class. Students benefit from seeing the high quality of writing that their peers can generate, and these collections of essays give instructors a ready and accessible supply of models to present to their students. These collections also reach the hands of those outside the University who are interested in learning more about the writing of college students.

One way to view college students' writing is to consider the goals for first-year writing course. At the University of Michigan these goals include the ability to make evidence-based arguments; read complex texts that support writing; use a variety of genres; develop awareness of strategies to use in different rhetorical situations; learn to organize, revise, edit, and proofread one's own writing; and collaborate with others to develop revision plans. As you read the selections included here, you will see evidence that students have attained these goals. You will also see how students have pushed the boundaries of some genres in their efforts to respond to varying rhetorical situations.

It is often said that the ability to write well is one of the most important attributes a college graduate can possess. Leaders in business, government, and non-profits all regularly lament the lack of writing ability among their employees, and hundreds of thousands of dollars are spent annually to help adult workers become more proficient writers. Providing college students with effective writing instruction is a much more expedient way to prepare future workers, and the essays in this collection display the writing abilities that first-year students can develop when their instructors have the professional knowledge and working conditions that enable them to teach student writers effectively. Students' writerly development does not, of course, conclude with completion of the first-year writing course, but this course provides the foundation upon which students can build as they move into other courses and contexts.

A collection like this depends upon the efforts of many different people. First among these are the writing instructors who show students how to do their best work, encourage them to push beyond what they think possible, and revise even after they think they are done. These instructors are also the ones who keep an eye out for outstanding writers in order to nominate them. Student nominees do additional revisions to make their submissions compelling. Dana Nichols, a member of the Sweetland faculty has for many years served as editor of these volumes. In this role she works with the Writing Prize Committee; recruits judges; coordinates the publication schedule and design with Aaron Valdez, Sweetland's Communications Coordinator; and proofreads the entire volume. Members of this year's Writing Prize Committee are Angie Berkeley, Jimmy Brancho, Cat Cassel, Raymond McDaniel, and Carol Tell. Judges for the First Year Writing Prize were Louis Cicciarelli, Lillian Li, Simone Sessolo, and Naomi Silver. I am deeply grateful to all of these individuals for making this collection possible, and I hope that you, dear reader, will find pleasure in seeing what student writers are able to do.

Anne Ruggles Gere
Director, Sweetland Center for Writing

The Rewards of First-Year Writing:

Introduction from the Chairs of the Feinberg Family Prize for Excellence in First-Year Writing

A prize for first-year writing is a funny thing. Thousands of students enter these introductory courses in writing with little expectation of a reward beyond the constructive feedback of their peers and instructors. Grades and writerly growth are supposed to be the good things that come to those who write in our composition courses—not *prizes*. If our own memories are any indication, the breathtaking pace of first-year composition can leave students feeling as though it is a considerable accomplishment simply to submit their papers on time.

Nevertheless, it is also the case that the students in our first-year writing courses regularly produce compositions that surprise and inspire those who read them—and that provide powerful models of what can be accomplished even in the space of a single course. We are delighted, then, to have the opportunity to introduce such a set of surprising and inspiring student writings—essays selected to receive the Feinberg Family Prize for Excellence in First-Year Writing. These essays embody the rewards of first-year writing and it is a delight to have the opportunity to reward them here.

While celebrating the essays that fill this volume, we want to celebrate also the dozens of essays nominated for this prize. The authors and nominating instructors for these essays are listed near the front of this volume, and we can personally attest that these essays portend promising futures for each writer nominated, and—taken together—reveal a writing program in which remarkable and rewarding instruction is taking place. Congratulations are due not just to the winning essays, but to all nominated writers and their nominating instructors. The richness of your efforts make the University of Michigan's English Department Writing Program what it is.

When reading the prize-winning essays collected here, it is important to remember that each comes to us through an ongoing process of discovery, drafting, and development. Each was partly shaped by the student peers who read and reviewed them, and proposed possibilities for revision. And each essay—while perhaps seeming to us a final, finished product—is better understood as one embodied point in an ongoing composing process. Were we to ask the authors of the essays collected here to continue this process of composing—perhaps by expanding or revising their essays for new audiences, or with the benefits of hindsight and new, hard-won insights—these essays would almost certainly emerge as different compositions from what you will read in the pages to follow.

In their present form, these essays represent three different explorations of argument, assuming different forms and addressing different topics. One, by Kara Semanision, offers an analytic argument in the form of an open-letter, taking on questions of institutional history and racism. Another, by Rose-Carmel Goddard, affords us a research-based object lesson on medical waste. And a third, by Hassan Bazzi, provides a narrative argument that explores the intersection of memory, culture, and the pieces of life affected war.

We hope that however you locate yourself relative to the writing classroom—as an instructor, student, administrator, or stakeholder—you will enlist these rewarding essays to enrich your engagements with writing. These essays can supply models for how to craft openings and conclusions, for staging a subtle argument, for marshalling evidence of several kinds. Each can also provide a staging ground for thinking through the complexities of process and rewriting. As you read these texts, ask yourself—*What about them do I find most rewarding? Imagine to your self—What rewarding addition or revision could I contribute to these essays?* Allow these essays to become part of your own writing process—part of your rewarding engagements with the world of first-year writing.

J. W. Hammond & Adrienne Raw
Graduate Student Mentors, English Department Writing Program

Piece of War
by Hassan Bazzi
From English 125
Nominated by R. Bruno

Hassan crafted this essay during a unit focused on reflective writing. During this unit, writers were asked to utilize a double perspective in order to narrativize past experiences with insight from their current perspective.

This is often a deceptively complicated assignment, as it can difficult to figure out a balance between writing in scene and reflective analysis. As you will observe, Hassan masterfully enmeshes timelines and techniques to craft an essay that is both beautiful and haunting.

The emotional tenor of this essay is buoyed by Hassan's deft writerly choices. In an earlier draft of this essay, Hassan included language that explicated meaning and moral for the audience. As he moved through the drafting process, Hassan replaced these telling constructions with sharp images and actions. He lets these moments stand as literary ghost notes that reshape the contract between author and audience.

R. Bruno

Piece of War

We go silent for a couple hours until we reach the mountains of Bint Jebail, which is where my father is from. I look to the left and covering the once beautiful mountains is a vast and terrifyingly dark smoke cloud, approaching us and consuming everything in its path. On the right, I see the face of my mother who is in utter shock. I also see my grandfather whose sweat drips faster than our favorite Brazilian soccer players, Kaka and Ronaldinho in primetime football. The airport had been bombed. His eyes were beaming, the sweat on his head, shinier than even the most luxurious diamond rings. With his cane held firmly in one hand, he releases a cold sigh in which his suspenders tighten, and his defeated look is all but certain. Stuck in the middle of the Lebanese-Israeli War in the summer of 2006, I was nine at the time, naïve and confused.

My grandpa was 6 feet 2 inches tall, used his special walking cane-- which was really just an ordinary wooden cane, and was overly concerned with his continued hair loss. Very outspoken and blunt, he was never afraid to speak his mind.

"Gido, does this mean we can't go home? He answers bluntly, "Skoot ya Hassan" (Shut up, Hassan). My grandfather and I had a strong and promising relationship, so my face suddenly flushed red, similarly to the time I ate my Amto Mona's fruit pizza for the first time. This was how I learned I was allergic to kiwi. Tears filled my eyes. My grandpa had never spoken to me that way. I was not aware of this at the time, but my grandpa loved being in control of everything in his life. He didn't like leaving anything to chance and certainly didn't believe in luck. The look on his face that night was the face of a man who had been stripped away of everything he had worked his life for.

***

5, 4, 3, 2, 1... Happy Birthday!! I walk into my home in Dearborn, Michigan to a surprise birthday party. I have just turned 13 years of age in February of 2010 and my family had invited all of my relatives and close friends.

My uncle Abbas was there sporting his classic Flowers by Renee T-shirt and jeans. My Amto Mona was there and she kept talking to my mom about how big I've gotten. Every relative, 23 or so, smile and congratulate me before returning to their own separate conversations. I observe balloons of every color, party plates and decorations, and so much food. Clearly, my family had conflicting ideas regarding where we would cater from. There was pizza from Jets, shish kabob platters from Al-Ameer, a couple of roasted chickens and three or four dozen fried pieces of whitefish with their crispy eyes darted straight at me. I paused for a second and wondered about the life of the fish I had been staring at. Had it fulfilled its purpose in life? I questioned whether it had moved on to another world or how it felt when it was forcefully plucked from the depths of the sea, searching endlessly for life, only to slowly discover it's looming reality. All this food was displayed in front of me and all that came to mind was the glaring innocent eyes of that $1.99 per pound whitefish that my cousin Hadi also had his eyes on. I'm sure he had intentions of eating it with some tartar sauce, lemon, and a hint of salt wrapped in some pita bread. On the island counter, I see all of the pastries that were brought; apple and pumpkin pies, fruit tarts, Eclairs, crème caramel, and a hidden cake with my name on it.

***

"Mama, I'm so hungry." I cry to my mother who is staring anxiously out the window. Maybe she was waiting for the rest of my family to arrive or maybe she was just afraid of another attack. "Hassan please be patient. When everybody arrives, you'll go with Yousef and Jesus down to the market to get some food." My mother wore beautiful and colorful scarves which were very common in our culture, had large brown eyes, perfectly precise arching eyebrows, and a beauty mark a couple centimeters above her lip, also found on the faces of my youngest sister and me. She was afraid, very much so, but I didn't know it. Two weeks had passed since the initiation of the war and we were hiding in a safe shelter in a small town 2 hour away from Beirut. Me and my sisters thought of it as staying at a hotel without all of our favorite amenities.

The rest of my relatives arrive, and we are immediately sent into the 'kids' room; a room with one bed was going to be shared with three of my sisters and four of my cousins. We all try to listen, and I decide to place my ear on the door, learning from Bill Nye the Science Guy that sounds travel fastest through solids. I hear weeping and intense arguing about what to do about the situation. And then instantly and spontaneously, complete and utter silence is upon us. My oldest cousin Yousef convinces us to slowly peak the door open. Breaking news appears on the small television set. It resembled something of a cardboard box that I paid no mind to and returned to my Nintendo DS to continue playing New Super Mario Bros. A warning is sent on the tv. More bombings are coming. I look up for a second and see a bloodied man without an arm on the tv and I quickly return my attention to Mario and his adventure. A couple hours later, the electricity goes out. With no water and no electricity, the unanimous decision is made to stay inside for the night. I sit in my bed, stomach growling in the dark, feeling the sticky sweat of my cousin transitioning from his body onto mine and I silently cry. Not because I am scared of the war but because I didn't understand.

****

"Hassan, I love your outfit!" My Amto Mona over-enthusiastically screams from across the room. "Thank you amto, my mom picked it out for me," I laugh. "Well your mom always did have the best sense of style." I awkwardly say thank you on her behalf to try and end the conversation. I was wearing a plaid red and black shirt from Express paired with some khakis. My hair was gelled to the side in a way that made me feel different but certainly wasn't my choice. "Hassan how did your soccer team do this year?" My aunt asks once more in an overly excited tone. I clearly know the she does not have any real interest as she displays her artificial smile, trying to make my mother proud. Half way into my answer, the lights dim and for a moment, my heart drops. The crowd breaks into a Happy Birthday song and I see the cake approach me. I see all of the eyes on me and I see the bright red flare from the candles. I get lost in the flare questioning its significance. The significance for any of this for that matter. I appreciated it and

I sure did blow out those candles, but with all those faces staring happily at me, I once again begin to cry, mistakenly taken for tears of joy by my close relatives.
****

"We must move quickly," my mom wakes us up in the middle of the night. I was hungry, tired, and so desperate for a shower. "Mama I want to go home." "We will Hassan, we will," my mom calmly says before I hear the calmness in her voice disappear as she says, "We are leaving the war." My grandpa drives us to a dock where one ship is present, boarding passengers. Before we leave, my grandpa gives me a kiss on the head which felt strange because my grandpa never engaged in such affectionate behavior. If I had known that was going to be the last time I saw my grandpa, I would've thought of something better to say than, "Bye Gido."

We quickly get on and are greeted by Cypriot men. Batista tightly grips my hand and says, "We'll get you all home soon." I sit in the seat next to my mother and my three sisters. I immediately notice the constant tidal movement the waves created under the boat. I think wow, this might actually be like a roller coaster ride. The ship sets for sail and my mom releases a sigh of relief, mistakenly thinking that we have escaped the war. 30 minutes in, the roller coaster's effects are felt. My younger sister, Nana, throws up on my mother's black long sleeve turtleneck. Batista hands my mother some paper towels and they go to the bathroom. The motion sickness doesn't end there. Six more people within the next 15 minutes puke and there is sudden panic on the boat. A woman falls to the ground and begins experiencing the effects of the seizure. Suddenly I am alone in the isle. I take out my Nintendo DS and continue playing Super Mario Bros. Eight hours later the ship docks and the beaming red light of an exit sign never looked more mesmerizing. We exit, and 50 people or so are taking pictures of us as if we're paparazzi, asking us to smile for the camera and interviewing others. I try returning to my DS, but it is now out of charge. My mother weeps and hugs us all. I had never seen my mother cry in front of me before. I didn't know what to feel. I hug her back and feel a cold shiver run down my spine.

****

"Hassan, smile!" My Amto Mona says as my cousins anxiously wait to take pictures with me. Three hours later, everybody leaves, and my mother and sisters are in bed. I take a warm shower, feeling the effects of every drop, and hoping that I am in control of how long it will last. I then wander into my bedroom and stretch my body across my bed, extending from end to end similar to my childhood favorite toy, Stretch Armstrong. I turn the lights off, close my eyes, and once again see the bloody man on the tv and the small safety shelter. I see my grandfather's eyes watching from the opposite end of the boarding ship and I wake up in sudden panic. There's a warm éclair resting on my bedside table. I'm too stuffed to eat, but I know my 9-year-old self wouldn't approve. I cut a piece of the éclair, observing the custard and chocolate layers, and uncomfortably begin chewing.

Surmounting the Struggle of Medical Waste
by Rose-Carmel Goddard

From English 125
Nominated by Cat Cassel

Rose-Carmel wrote this essay for my Health Science Scholars Program English 125. This assignment takes inspiration from a real world publishing genre, the "Object Lesson" essay series in The Atlantic, where authors examine "the hidden lives of ordinary things" and "develop original insights around and novel lessons about the object in question." Rose-Carmel certainly accomplishes that task in her piercing analysis of the environmental effects of medical waste. As her reader, I feel like I've been taught something about objects I had not given serious consideration to before--individually shrink-wrapped toothbrushes, for example. Her careful research yields surprising insights--for instance, the link between the rise of disposable, and particularly plastic, medical devices and panicked response to sterility and hygiene during the AIDS crisis. She swiftly positions herself as a credible authority on the subject as a person once responsible for keeping disposable objects stocked in a hospital, and proposes several concrete and seemingly compelling solutions for her reader as well.

Cat Cassel

Surmounting the Struggle of Medical Waste

For a year I walked around the hospital as a quiet shadow: dutiful and aware of my responsibilities while everyone else passed by in a whirl of activity. The medical surgery floor buzzed with residents making their way through rounds, nurses pushing drugs with ambiguous and complicated side effects, and a grumpy floor administrator who barely gave me a nod as I walked onto the floor, 4G, every Tuesday at 4 pm. Unnoticed and unassuming, I went about my work as a hospital volunteer under my own authority and direction. My main rules to follow were not to get into the way of the doctors and nurses, to make sure the patients were comfortable in any way I could help them, and to restock the supply closets outside of each patient room. In order to keep the hallway supply closets adequately full, I found myself running in and out of the two central supply rooms on 4G quite frequently. As odd as it may sound, these vast supply rooms, tucked into the heart of 4G, were uniquely fascinating to me. Their towering shelves were overflowing with supplies from unfamiliar medical equipment, to common toiletry items for patients such as shampoo or a toothbrush. Among this maze of supplies, I spent my time organizing, sorting, and retrieving the necessities for which 4G needed out on the floor to serve their patients. Yet among the wide-ranging diversity of all the supplies and equipment in these rooms, there was one common factor: everything was disposable. Every medical tool, from the syringes, to the respirator kits, and even the toothbrushes were encapsulated in their own set of intricate layers of plastic and paper, all of it to be thrown out after one use. Almost nothing in this closet was reusable and would swiftly end up accumulating in the landfill of medical waste shortly after the transient role it played in aiding a health practitioner in the treatment of a patient.

The shift from relying on reusable or reprocessed medical devices to one-time-use disposable tools is a somewhat recent transition. Previously, most medical devices were made out of durable materials such as metal, glass, or rubber. These medical devices were sterilized and reused patient after patient. Around the

1980s, medical professionals started relying more heavily on disposable medical devices made out of plastic that were made to be used once and then thrown away. This push was partly due to the onset of the HIV epidemic that made health care practitioners wary of reusing medical devices due to fear of infection (Chen). Thus, the disposable nature of the instruments and devices in the medical field did not come about without reason. Disposable medical supplies, primarily made of plastics, are commonly used today because of their maintenance of sterility, versatility, and convenience.

One of the main reasons plastic medical equipment is so useful is because it is easy to keep disposable materials sterile for patient care. Once a device or piece of equipment has been used, it can be thrown out with ease, without having to sterilize it again under the strict protocols required for reuse or reprocessing of medical instruments. The key factor to an effective barrier of infectious and pathogenic microbes is to ensure medical instruments packaging does not have any holes or breaks in the sterile boundary between the medical device and the outside world ("Maintenance of Sterility"). Items such as plastic dialysis tubes and disposable syringes are used to eliminate the fear of transmitting blood-borne infections, such as HIV or hepatitis B, through medical devices that come into contact with human blood. With reusable syringes in particular, there is risk of potential laceration when capping the needle. In addition, if syringes are not re-sterilized properly, it may cause the transfer of infectious diseases (North and Halden). Medical devices made up of disposable materials eliminate the time and strict protocols needed to sterilize medical instruments again, and thus contribute to both efficiency of care and patient safety.

Different types of plastic polymers are used to engineer a broad variety of medical devices, such as prosthetics, synthetic tissues, and even micro-needle patches for drug delivery. Absorbable sutures are yet another innovate example that are made up of biodegradable plastic polymers that will biodegrade in a patient's body at a certain rate depending on the needs of the patient based on their surgery. This technology reduces the number of surgeries a patient must undergo, since the sutures or other implanted medical devices will biodegrade at a certain point and do not need surgical removal. Along with these unique innovations, plastic medical devices are also a huge part of everyday patient care in a hospital setting. For example, disposable items such as latex gloves and intravenous (IV) bags and tubing are used extremely frequently by health care practitioners and are regarded highly for their convenience. (North and Halden). When going into a patient room, health care practitioners simply need to put on a clean, new pair of plastic gloves to examine and care for their patient. Leaving the room, they effortlessly can slip the gloves off, along with any germs or bacteria picked up in the patient room, and slip them into the trash, never to be used again. With a similar level of importance, IV bags and tubing are used to immediately replace fluids in dehydrated patients, as well as immediate drug delivery, blood transfusions, and to correct imbalances in electrolytes in patients both quickly and efficiently. IV bags are essential in delivering these treatments and provide a convenient way for health practitioners to correct precarious physiological levels in their patients with speed and efficiency (North and Halden). Evidently, medical devices made out of disposable plastic polymers have an important role in health care and have allowed for a lot of innovation for a diverse range of patient treatments.

Although the effectiveness of plastic medical devices cannot be denied, disposable medical products are creating a huge cost on the environment. Colossal amounts of medical waste are accumulated in the health care system from disposable medical products. As of 2013, the healthcare industry reported 3.4 billion pounds of waste annually, 850 million pounds of that waste being purely made up of plastic materials (North and Halden). Shockingly, a large majority of the items disposed of are left unopened and untouched and are thrown away for simply being brought into a patient room or operating room. For starters, it is important to note the significant amount of petroleum consumption used in the production of these plastic materials to begin with. Secondly, a large majority of this medical waste ends up in landfills, where none of the energy or material used to make these disposable medical devices can be recovered (North and

Halden). Another method of disposing of medical waste is through incineration. This method of disposal is beneficial in that it aids the prevention of disease transmission, the medical waste does not end up taking space in landfills, and there is some recovery of the energy used to produce the devices initially through the process of incineration. Unfortunately, incineration can become harmful due to the release of carcinogenic air toxins upon disposal of the materials. The environmental costs of disposable medical products need to be considered upon use of these devices due to their seriously harmful side effects.

Another issue with the mass disposal of medical devices is the hefty dollar amount wasted on the materials that are used once or are thrown away before they can be used at all. In Marshall Allen's article "What Hospitals Waste", he cited that the annual cost of the medical waste in 2012 was estimated by the National Academy of Medicine to be $765 billion dollars per year. Another estimate by the researchers at San Francisco Medical Center approximated the hospital wasted $2.9 million dollars in neurosurgery supplies in a single year alone (Allen). Allen interviewed a registered nurse, Elizabeth McLellan, who was appalled by the amount of wasted medical supplies she witnessed at the hospital and started collecting the unused items instead. In 2009, McLellan founded a nonprofit called Partners for World Health to maximize her efforts to reduce medical waste. The warehouses of Partners for World Health are filled to the brim of untouched medical supplies that would otherwise be thrown away before they were ever used. Among these medical treasures procured from hospitals that intended to discard these unused medical devices are boxes filled with $129 feeding bags with an expiration date of August 2019, unexpired Ethicon sutures each $431 per box, and bipolar forceps priced at $299. In 2016, Partners for World Health sent seven containers of the collected medical supplies overseas to hospitals and medical clinics in need. Each of the containers were worth roughly $250,000 and weighed in at 15,000 pounds. Some other pieces of medical equipment that the organization has collected and sent overseas are a $25,000 ultrasound machine, an infant warming machine worth $3,995, and a dozen trocars (a type of surgical instrument) each worth $4,400 (Allen). McLellan describes that most of the items are unused in hospitals and collected by the organization because they fall into the following categories: "equipment discarded for upgraded models, supplies tossed after a hospital changed vendors, or materials donated by the families of patients who have died. Other items are past their expiration dates or were swept out by strict infection control procedures but remain safely usable" (Allen). The work done by Partners for World Health is just one organization that demonstrates the amount of medical supplies wasted by the American Healthcare system. There are several other nonprofits doing similar work, and still yet, millions more pounds of unused medical supplies that is sent straight to landfills. The financial burden of this margin of waste is far too great to be ignored without a plan of action.

From large scale systematic changes to day-to-day modifications in typical methods of operation, there are several adjustments that can, and should be made to address this surmounting problem of excessive waste. In the research field of biodegradable plastics, recent innovation of a new biodegradable plastic polymer has the potential to replace some of the harmful plastics used in medical supplies. This polymer would not only reduce human exposure to BPA, but would avoid millions of metric tons of carbon dioxide emissions released into the environment (North and Halden). Knowing that the use of plastics in medical supplies cannot be entirely eliminated from hospitals, it is important to consider alternative plastics and disposable products as substitutes of the materials associated with harmful health effects on both some patient populations and the environment.

Another necessary adjustment for the health care industry is to use more reusable medical supplies versus disposable medical devices that are used once and then thrown away. According to Emily North and Rolf Halden in their article, "Plastics and Environmental Health: The Road Ahead", "it is now becoming more cost-effective to switch to reusable alternatives" from disposable plastic products and "has been estimated to potentially result in a 50% reduction of medical equipment costs". With this in mind, the initial higher cost of reusable medical equipment compared to the disposable plastic alternatives actually pays off in the overall timeline. For example, one hospital exchanged their blue polypropylene wrap that is used for maintaining the sterility of the surgical tools in the operating room with reusable surgical hard cases. Due to this change, the hospital saved $51,000 annually (North and Halden). By choosing to use reusable alternatives in place of disposable plastic medical equipment, a large dent can be put in the amount of medical waste being thrown out of hospital and subsequently save some money for the hospital as well.

In matters of daily procedures, something as simple as only bringing the necessary medical supplies to the operating room that will be used for the specific procedure can have significant effects on reducing waste. Better communication between the surgeon and OR nurses helps to specify what will be used for the procedure, in order to limit the unnecessary items that are thrown out. Communication with medical product vendors is also valuable in order to consolidate packaged surgical kits by eliminating the extraneous items that are not needed for particular surgeries. Health practitioners at the University of Minnesota Medical Center, reviewed 38 different varieties of operating room packages to analyze what could be eliminated. The team reduced the packages to almost half of the original amount, resulting in a drop of $50 in supply costs and one pound less of trash per procedure (Chen). Reducing unneeded materials is not an ultimate fix but is a step that can be implemented instantaneously to streamline the amount of supplies wasted. With better communication between colleagues in the operating room and medical supply vendors, medical waste can be reduced in a fairly simple and straightforward manner.

Enacting methods of avoiding harmful plastics and finding alternatives is a good start at reducing the amount of medical waste, but it is not enough on its own. In order make the system around medical supplies run more efficiently, it is essential to reconfigure the central ways of thinking around disposable medical products in the health care field. Although disposable, plastic forms of medical equipment are valued for their convenience, low initial cost, sterility, and versatility, it is not acceptable to stick with the current practices when the "long-term harm clearly outweighs any short-term benefits realized" (North and Halden). Convenience is not an excuse to squander both money and usable medical supplies in the American Health Care system. Thus, hospital protocols must be restructured in order to address the environmental and financial burdens medical waste is causing.

Work Cited

Allen, M arshall. "What Hospitals Waste." *ProPublica*, ProPublica, 9 Mar. 2017, www.propublica.org/article/what-hospitals-waste.

Chen, Ingfei. "In World of Throwaways, Making a Dent in Medical Waste." *The New York Times*, The New York Times, 5 July 2010, www.nytimes.com/2010/07/06/health/06waste.html.

"Maintenance of Sterility." *Sterile Barrier Association*, www.sterilebarrier.org/general-public/maintenance-of-sterility/.

North, Emily J., and Rolf U. Halden. "Plastics and Environmental Health: the Road Ahead." *Reviews on Environmental Health*, vol. 28, no. 1, Jan. 2013, pp. 1–8., doi:10.1515/reveh-2012-0030.

Power and Pedagogy: An Open Letter on C.C. Little
by Kara Semanision
From English 125
Nominated by Katherine Hummel

In keeping with our ENGL 125 class's theme of "Place, Privilege, and Belonging," Kara took the open letter assignment as an opportunity to interrogate U-M's institutional memory surrounding C.C. Little, a past U-M president and noted eugenicist. She exceeded every expectation for the assignment; her essay is well-researched, nuanced, persuasive, and generously acknowledges counterarguments. Calling explicitly for the removal of Little's name from the science building, Kara expertly analyzes the U-M Board of Regents' own policy language to interrogate its relevance in light of her meticulous research on Little's racist, sexist, and ableist politics.

Kara's piece is remarkable for the high levels of sophistication, eloquence, and confidence that characterize her writing. She respectfully acknowledges her audience's expertise while challenging the Regents to demonstrate their commitment to diversity, equity, and inclusion by grappling with Little's legacy. In doing so, Kara makes legible the material consequences of institutional blind spots, connecting U-M to other universities facing similar calls for removing problematic honorifics. Reading her essay in the aftermath of the Regents' decision to remove Little's name only raises the stakes of her argument further. Allying herself with those subject to ableism, racism, and sexism at the university, Kara uses this assignment to do much more than receive a high grade: she amplifies the voices of marginalized communities and speaks truth to power.

Katherine Hummel

Power and Pedagogy: An Open Letter on C.C. Little

Dear University of Michigan Board of Regents,

Just over a year ago, you were issued a document detailing principles to considered in the interpretation of existing name-changing procedure for buildings. The document, released by the President's Advisory Committee on University History at the request of President Schlissel, came in response to collective outcry from students, faculty, and community members alike over the namesake of one building in particular. I scarcely even have to reference the name, you know it. The place in your mind where it lives is sore. Not nearly so sore, though, as the place it lives in the minds of those crying for change. Those who feel the sting of the man whose name has become a geographical reference on campus. Those who know what the prioritization of his legacy entails. Those who know that the name Clarence Cook Little means that racism, sexism, elitism, and ableism are far from dead at the University of Michigan.

I am sure you are aware of those factors of Clarence Cook Little's life and academic presence that make the presence of his name at the forefront of a place of learning and scientific research inappropriate. The eugenics movement, which encouraged state-mandated sterilization of those labeled unfit to have children because of alleged 'feeblemindedness', is without dispute an unspeakable violation of human rights. The State, citing pseudo scientific evidence provided by people like Little, did irreversible damage to about 60,000 individuals nationally (Kaelber). Within the state of Michigan, victims were four times more likely to be black than white, and much more likely to be Native American. Similar racial trends were seen across the country, as well as trends of increased sterilization rates among LGBTQ and impoverished people (Kaelber). The ideology of the eugenics movement, you will remember, was also the basis of the xenophobic beliefs which set the Holocaust in motion. Given that these factors have not yet been rendered worthy of your power to make positive change here, I will speak briefly on Clarence Cook Little's history and association with the University of Michigan.

Little was born in Massachusetts in 1888. He was educated at Harvard, and there began his research in genetics. He researched subjects such as Mendelian inheritance, transplant success and rejection, and cancer. In 1919, Little became a research associate and assistant director at the Station for Experimental Evolution, Carnegie Institution. This lab, specializing in genetic experiments on plants and animals, had been shaped into a center for eugenic research by Charles Davenport, a leader of the movement. In its early days, a newspaper article titled "To Improve the Race" described the station as a place with the "Object of deducing laws to eliminate defectives from our race" (Gerould).

Little became president of the University of Maine in 1922, and then left to become president of the University of Michigan in 1925. His tenure here was short, lasting only four years, the last of which overlapped with his presidency of the American Eugenics Society. His involvement with the Society was not limited to the end of his time as president here. He was the director of the AES from 1923-1939, and thereby is liable to have served their interests for the entirety of his tenure at the University of Michigan. After leaving the University in 1929, Little moved to Bar Harbor, Maine to continue his research career, as well as carry on with the AES. Additionally, he served as the managing director of the American Society for the Control of Cancer until 1945. In 1954, Little became Scientific Director for the Scientific Advisory Board of the Council for Tobacco Research. He remained there until his death, suffering a heart attack at age 83 (Goldman).

The Board of Regent's 2008 "Policy for Naming of Facilities, Spaces, and Streets" states that the merit of an honorific naming of a place is valid if the individual has "had University-wide influence, or the individual has made exceptional contributions to the nation or world" (Policy for Naming). This has been your main argument for maintaining this honorific naming. Let me address Little's. exceptional contributions to the world. Yes, he is documented in many scientific contexts as a leader and prominent researcher. It should also be noted that this literature largely avoids his involvement in the eugenics movement.

Mendelian genetic research, yes. But bear in mind that it was conducted at a facility whose mission statement was to "deduce laws to eliminate defectives from our race". Bear in mind that it was commissioned by Charles Davenport, a eugenist whose research assumed the guise of legitimate science to perpetuate racist and ableist ideals (Gerould). Most of all, bear in mind that research conducted here not only went on to fuel eugenist rhetoric in the United States, but in genocide and ethnic cleansing efforts around the world.

Yes, Little served as the managing director of the American Society for the Control of Cancer, later to become the American Cancer Society. He served a crucial role in the early days of an organization which went on to greatly increase awareness, knowledge, and research activity in the fight against cancer. But not long after his time at the ASCC, he fought directly against its efforts to bring to light tobacco's carcinogenic nature. Serving as chairman of the Tobacco Industry Research Committee, Little, despite his expansive research on cancer and carcinogens, perpetuated the message that there was "no conclusive scientific proof of a link between smoking and cancer" (Brandt). Though this was common industry-pushed propaganda at the time, even his colleagues spoke out in surprise at his stance. "It seems astonishing to me that a man of his eminence in the field of cancer and genetics would condescend to take a position like that", said Evarts Graham, a leading thoracic surgeon of the time (Brandt). While Little's research might have been productive, he worked in direct opposition to its possible altruistic outcomes.

It is also important to take into account Little's more local legacy. In his short tenure, he made pushes for more student housing. He also instituted "Freshman Week", an early version of Welcome Week (Goldman). Both are positive contributions that last to this day. I do not discount their merit, but ask you to consider those students he sought to extend these privileges to. Little's stance on rights to education was well-known among colleagues as elitist, even for the times. His controversial policy on education was defined first and foremost by his belief that "only those students deemed able to make the best use of education should be admitted to universities" (Little). Extrapolating from Little's commitment to popular eugenic standards, "able" is likely to have meant students of western European descent who came from backgrounds of affluence. This meant that every good work of his at this university, while fruitful today, were not intended to benefit who they have. I understand the appeal of emphasising the positive results of Little's presidency here, but his actions, even if beneficial to a select group of people, cannot be separated from his motives.

Our President, Mark Schlissel himself, said that "in some cases, changing a name may be less important than providing adequate interpretation of it" (Fitzgerald). I am not in disagreement, interpretation largely determines public opinion. Judging, however, by breadth of information on Little, efforts made by this board and the University to make available reasons Little's name should be allowed to remain have been unconvincing. A simple search for the name Clarence Cook Little yields a limited range of results. The first page, outside of a wikipedia entry, is composed entirely of editorials and historical evidence calling to attention his "dark past" and "strange career". Feel free to try yourselves. Try and see from an objective viewpoint. Anyone not searching deeply for some flash of good or resisting the removal of his name will certainly encounter first the dark shadow that Little's legacy casts over our university. The name change of this building would also provide the University an opportunity to reconsider how it interprets the success of its distinguished alumni and faculty who are people of color. Currently, the interpretation seems to be that only one building, the Trotter Multicultural Center, should be named for a person of color (Slagter). This interpretation is far from adequate.

I do not make light the importance of due process. You and a board of your peers, the President's Advisory Committee on University History, have carefully compiled a straightforward set of guidelines for potential review of university space names. Thank you for making this document fair and accessible to the public and the students; it emphasises your devotion to an open, free flowing dialogue between the university and its community members. I do not presume to be as well versed on the topic as yourselves, but feel that my view truly reflects the perspective of much of the student body and involved public body. In this capacity, I will address the Committee's relevant principles in relation to the C. C. Little Science Building.

First is the principle of pedagogy. Here it is declared that our naming process, as well as its result, should be a way of learning about our past, exceptional contributions by our faculty and alumni, acts of generosity, or important administrative influence (McDonald). It could be argued that Clarence Cook Little presents an opportunity to learn. My peers and I do not suggest that we forget him; it is important that history is learned from if it cannot be celeb rated. In my initial statement of grounds, I presented some of Little's contributions and influential policies. I feel that the circumstances presented in parallel should define these legacies as not a history of excellence or generosity, but as a cautionary tale of science without evidence or humanity. The conflict is not that Little's name remains in our history, that is something we must stay vigilant of. We must also, though, be vigilant that the remembrance of his name is not one that can be called honorific.

Now comes the principle of interpretation. Defined here are the following principles: the name of a building does not fade in meaning after its naming ceremony, and continued and re-evaluated interpretation are necessary, as well as potential education on why a name remains (McDonald). The non-editorial literature provided by the University is strangely sunny in tone considering the man it is describing. In the official Presidential Profiles of the Faculty History Project, there is no mention of Little's involvement in eugenics or with the tobacco lobby (Peckham). As a student of neuroscience and psychology at the University of Michigan, and someone with a strong understanding of Little's history, my interpretation of his name is not so pleasant. Less pleasant are the opinions of those groups his work disproportionately oppressed and dehumanized. In the state of Michigan, and even within the University Hospital, at least 3,786 residents, largely of Native American and African American descent or marginalized sexuallity, were involuntarily sterilized (Millikan). I suggest that the interpretation of Little's legacy currently upheld by the University is reckoned with the interpretation by the public and the student body, and re-evaluated before consideration in the conversation on name change. This is not to say that the opinion of the faculty is unimportant or uninformed, but the voice of an overwhelmingly white and male cohort cannot be the only one heard in a dialogue on systematic oppression.

The principle of due diligence. Exhaustive research and evaluation of the public record (McDonald). You, having been asked time and again to reconsider the name of this space, are doubtlessly well-educated on the subject. There is almost no better place to look at records of Little than here, where he served. If this research has not been enough to justify removal of the name, I ask of you to research the legacy of not only the Little name, but the spiderweb of scars left by the causes he stood for. The state of Michigan, you will find, is the only state which had sterilization laws, and has yet to issue an apology to its victims (Millikan). If we cannot acknowledge the harm that found momentum here, how can we fight to alleviate its ongoing sting? If it is not clear that Little is a burden to students here, let us look to the more present hurt of those who share his ideology. The same rhetoric that fuels the likes of Charles Murray and Richard Spencer fueled the cause Little left this university to pursue. These men have incited violence and unrest, even brought death to those who oppose their ideology (Svrluga). As well as researching the past, we must research the current reaches of the oppression associated with Little.

We have arrived at the principle of commitment. The University owes to the namesake, donor, or honoree a high level of commitment and appropriate attention from the Vice President and the General Counsel, who will enforce the 2008 Policy and Guidelines regarding named spaces (McDonald). The C. C. Little Science Building was named by the Board of Regents in 1968, long past Little's life but long before much understanding of its lasting impacts. You, the current Board, have been presented with an opportunity to display the University's commitment to justice, progress, and inclusion. Assembling a committee representing groups impacted by the work of Little and his peers, like Victor Vaughan and William W. Cook, shows the face of the University as one committed to betterment over stagnance. Though a committee has been assembled in the past, and agreed that the name should be changed, it remains the same (Slagter). This is not the commitment you have been advised to display, but a blatant violation of it.

On the note of stagnance, I reference the principle of revision, which allows for change in interpretation to prompt change in representation. Though there is not much precedence of name change at the University of Michigan, the President's Advisory Committee on University History encourages modern discourse and action on antiquated views (McDonald). With this in mind, we look to our peers in the academic and scientific communities. Universities such as Yale, and its Calhoun College, are also being faced with calls for action. Universities such as the University of Maryland and Georgetown University have garnered respect for answering the call, ousting the names Byrd and Mulledly, respectively (Stern). Revision does not bring the shame of past principle down upon our heads, rather lifts from our shoulders the burdens of moving them forward with us.

The prospect of change brings us to the principle of consistency. Here, there is an addendum to the principle of commitment (McDonald). Though commitment is owed to a namesake, the PACUH has brought to light that this principle, without allowance for name review, would mean that process of honoring by name is nearly at an end and reflects the largely white, male body of administration that was present here in the University's earlier years. Do the "leaders and citizens who will challenge the present and enrich the future", as proclaimed in our mission statement, not include people of all races, genders, and creeds (Mission and Integrity)? If we are to fight the narrative of white, male dominance in academia and truly represent all who are leaders, we must seize the opportunity to make the achievements of an intersectional community as visible as possible.

Drawing on all of the above principles is the principle of contemporary effect. "Honorifics given at one time can have significantly different effects on community members at another and these too are worthy of consideration" (McDonald). I implore you to hear our community's suffering under the name C. C. Little. The same groups attacked by racist vandalism, demographic exclusion, the real and present threats presented by speakers like Charles Murray and Richard Spencer, feel, in no small way, the sting of Little's legacy. Your current position, as the leading and speaking body of this institution, has also placed the burden of proof and process on these already overburdened groups. Despite the weight on their shoulders, they have done all they can to reach out to you and share with you their view of the Little name on a building of legitimate scientific education and research. Please listen, if not for the sake of your student body, for your promise to uphold our mission statement.

How can we enact our visionary tenants of promotion and celebration of diversity and acceptance of challenge and change if we ourselves do not operate under them? How can we celebrate ideals that have cost so many their fundamental human rights, both on American soil and in every other nation which has borne witness to genocide and atrocity on the basis of biological essentialism? History lies in the hands of the powerful. I, supported by the voices of thousands of community members, urge you to use your power to show that this history of hate and injustice is not to be honored, but learned from. Stop celebrating the name and actions of Clarence Cook Little, or be left behind and disparaged with his xenophobic worldview. Remove his name from its place of honor on our Science Building, and replace it with one that can begin to heal our community.

Works Cited

Brandt, Allan M. "Inventing Conflicts of Interest: A History of Tobacco Industry Tactics." *American Journal of Public Health*, no. 1, ser. 102, Jan. 2012, pp. 63-71. US National Library of Medicine, doi:https://dx.doi.org/10.2105%2FAJPH.2011.300292.

"C. C. Little Building Name Change Request." University of Michigan Faculty.

Fitzgerald, Rick. "U-M defines principles, process for building renaming requests." *The University Record*, The University of Michigan, 23 Jan. 2017, record. umich.edu/articles/u-m-defines-principles-process-building-renaming-requests.

Gerould, John H. "Article on founding of Station for Experimental Evolution referring to eugenic prospects." *DNA Learning Center*, Cold Springs Harbor Laboratory, www.dnalc.org/view/10512-Article-on-founding-of-Station-for-Experimental-Evolution-referring-to-eugenic-prospects. html.

Goldman, Karla. "Looking A Little More Deeply Into C. C. Little." *Liberal Arts in the Moment*, University of Michigan, 25 Sept. 2017, sites.lsa.umich. edu/learn-speak-act/201 7/09/25/looking-a-little-more-deeply-into-c-c-little /.

Kaelber, Lutz. "Michigan." *Eugenics: Compulsory Sterilization in 50 States*, University of Vermont, 2010, www.uvm.edu/~lkaelber/eugenics/MI/ MI.html.

Little, Clarence Cook. "Clarence Cook Little Papers," *Bentley Historical Library*, University of Michigan, quod.lib.umich.edu/b/bhlead/umich-bhl-851744?view=text.

McDonald, Terrence J. "Committee Views on Possible Review of University Space Names." University of Michigan, 6 Jan. 2017.

Millikan, Arikia. "A Dark Medical History." *The Michigan Daily*, The University of Michigan, 12 Feb. 2008, www.michigandaily.com/content/arikia-millikan-dark-medical-history.

"Mission and Integrity." *Accreditation*, University of Michigan, 2010, www.accreditation.umich.edu/mission/.

"Policy for Naming of Facilities, Spaces and Streets." University of Michigan, May 2008.

Slagter, Martin. "UMich protesters demand change of building name honoring ex-President." *MLive*, MLive Media Group, 28 Sept. 2017, www.mlive.com/news/ann-arbor/index.ssf/2017/09/umich_students_call_for_name_c.html.

Stern, Alexandra. "Why the C. C. Little Building Should Be Renamed." *Liberal Arts in the Moment*, University of Michigan College of Literature, Science, and the Arts, 22 Sept. 2017, sites.lsa.um ich.edu/leam-speak-act/2017/09/22/why-the-c-c-little-building-should-be-renamed/.

Svrluga, Susan. "'Kill Them': Three Men Charged in Shooting after Richard Spencer Speech." *The Washington Post*, Fred Ryan, 20 Oct. 2017, www.washingtonpost.com/news/grade-point/wp/2017/10/20/kill-them-three-men-charged-in-shooting-after-richard-spencer-speech/?noredirect=on.

Introduction to the Matt Kelley Prize for Excellence in First-Year Writing, Excellence in Multilingual Writing Prize, and the Excellence in the Practice of Writing Prize

On behalf of the Sweetland Center for Writing I am pleased to congratulate Kate Glad and Aditya Ravi, winners of the Matt Kelley Prize for Excellence in First-Year Writing; Xuanwen Huang and Zhiyoa Zhang, winners of the Excellence in Multilingual Writing Prize; and Michelle Karls and Tigran Terterian, winners of the Excellence in the Practice of Writing Prize. Our judges were impressed by the innovative and creative ways in which students responded to their instructors' assignments. Our winners distinguished themselves by crafting delightful essays that inform, persuade, and inspire.

We thank instructors for nominating their students and designing classes that encourage writers to produce their best work. I am grateful to my colleagues in the Sweetland Center for Writing who served as judges for this year's first-year writing prizes: Louis Cicciarelli, Lillian Li, Shuwen Li, Simone Sessolo, and Naomi Silver. I am especially grateful to Angie Berkley, Jimmy Brancho, Cat Cassel, Raymond McDaniel and Carol Tell, who volunteered to serve as members of the writing prize committee and graciously accepted extra reading and tie-breaking duties. My sincere thanks to Laura Schuyler, who guides the writing prizes from beginning to end, and to Aaron Valdez, who produces these beautiful volumes. We hope you enjoy reading these essays as much as we did.

Dana Nichols
Lecturer, Sweetland Center for Writing

Kelly Prize for Excellence in First-Year Writing

Chuck Too Close
by Catherine Glad
From CompLit 122: The Aesthetic Configurations of Life
Nominated by Duygu Ergun

In this essay, the student chose to work with an artwork by a well-known artist in New York, who was accused of sexual harassment by the models he worked with. It is an exemplary close reading, where the student interprets the artist's close-up style, use of the sense of intimacy and vulnerability in his depictions of the subjects, and the public exhibitions of his work in subways as part of a cultural analysis of how his continuous sexual harassment is covered up through his alleged brilliance as an artist.

Duygu Ergun

Chuck Too Close

Twelve murals by artist Chuck Close went up in the New York subway system in 2010. You can find portraits by Close not only in the train station but in museums everywhere. He works with celebrities like supermodel Kate Moss and his acquaintances who model as a favor. His process is simple. Using a macro lens, he takes extreme close-ups of a subject's face. Then, he renders the photos as huge paintings, murals, or collages.

Sometimes he works on capturing a face, precisely. Transcribing wrinkles, scars, and freckles wrought with detail. Other times he takes artistic liberty and abstracts his portraits in various art styles. But the fact remains; it's always—save a few exceptions—a giant face. Close's work runs on intimacy and the vague unease that comes from having such a large face imposed on the viewer. Chuck Close's work works because he gets so close. He thrives in the uncomfortable; his nine-foot tall canvases loom above us and make us wonder what the model is thinking, if the model ever suddenly remembers the throngs of voyeurs who go to museums to stare at them, or how they felt in the studio with the giant camera lens a few inches from their nose.

One giant face is of fellow artist Cecily Brown; you can find her at the Second and Eighty-sixth Street stop of the red line (Artnet). She is the mosaic right next to exit 2A. Most of her face is comprised of small round tiles in peach or brown shades. They carve out the shape of her nose, a row of about five of the dark ones make up her eyelashes. But in the mire of dots when the mosaic is cropped in on just her left eye, there are two small round tiles that are neither a shade of peach nor brown. One is pink and one is blue. They hold no information about Cecily. Instead, they are a mark that this art is *art*. Art made by an artist—someone who tiled this wall and through their own creative intuition placed a blue tile under her eye and a pink one on her cheekbone. Two circles that break the continuity of Cecily. They serve some purpose other than showing the viewer a face. These tiles are a license taken by Chuck Close to mark the face of his subject in the way he sees fit. A pink tile and a blue tile that might as well be a signature on a birthday card and a fingerprint taken by police.

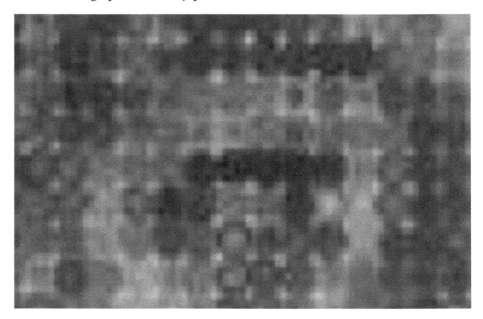

Although they hold no information about Cecily they say a lot about Chuck. Barely interrupting her face, the pink tile mildly highlights Cecily's cheekbone. A kind impression meant to complement, like light makeup. It shows the care and the craftsmanship put into Close's art. It shows his dedication to his craft and the multiple years one piece can take. In that interruption, there are thousands of polaroids digitally blown up and painstakingly committed to canvas or tile. Several artistic styles are lovingly represented here, his early photo-realistic work and his kaleidoscopic later paintings, his brief foray into pop art, and, of course, his homage to Roman murals with his New York subway work. It's a lifetime of dedication to art and the well-deserved respect of his peers and critics.

But the blue tile harshly interrupts and tells a different story. Positioned just on the lower lash line, it's not a tear, although it could almost be one. Unlike the pink tile that holds decades, this blue one holds two discrete days. It's not Chuck's story or Cecily's, but two women artist's—currently working artist Julia Fox and an unnamed woman who was a graduate art student at the time. Both women were asked by Close to model for him and were honored to join the ranks of artists he felt worthy to make giant. But when they arrived at his studio, they were asked to undress and pose nude. Close has shown nudes before in galleries, in fact, one of his images of the aforementioned Kate Moss is a nude. But his signature is not full body nudes, it is famously just of the face. His series featuring fellow artists, that this Cecily painting is part of that these women thought they would be featured in, is especially not nude. Neither woman actually let him photograph them, as the encounters turned predatory after they undressed. He commented on their bodies and offered them money before telling them to leave after they did not reciprocate these remarks and actions. Empowered by #metoo, Julia Fox went to *The New York Times* and *The Huffington Post* with the events of one afternoon with him and the unnamed woman soon followed.

Although the particular painting of Cecily I am close reading was made in 2010 and she has never spoken about such an experience, this bright pseudo-tear still holds these allegations from 2007 and 2013. It explodes the process of meaning making from the inside by absorbing, once real life actions were brought to light, the degree of license and entitlement claimed by Close. Because that is how art works—nothing is really done being painted and the grout on the tiles of the mosaics in the 86th street subway stop is never fully set. If the artist evolves, our perception of their art must as well. The subway tiles in our mind have to rearrange themselves to show us where the small interruptions are hiding and the large ones we cannot ignore. A tile that once said nothing, that was blue just for the sake of being blue, that interrupted the portrait just to interrupt, now holds the trauma of two women. This tile now says that while they were nude, Close invaded their personal space and made sexual comments until they were so uncomfortable and unsafe that they left.

Inside this overtly discontinuous tile is a new meaning of Close. A new meaning for the uneasy feelings he spent his career cultivating. After years of being asked by Close to consider what it means to be intimate and truly see a person, we now have a moral imperative to examine him the way we have been examining people through his eyes for years. We must consider him more closely and we must consider what it is that Close means by close.

When this forced intimacy was purely artistic, a minorly discontinuous tile on the cheekbone so to speak, Close was lauded as a genius. It was brilliant for him to use a camera to invade personal space, with the consent of the model, as an artistic endeavor. To make us ask those questions about what models think and how they feel being seen. When he did that, he was pushing the envelope—it was exciting. But that is not the real world. That was an artistic realm where evocation of a feeling is not the same as the infliction of one. So we ask again what does the model think and how do they feel being seen, but now we know how they feel and nothing about is genius or exciting anymore. The model is afraid.

There is a line between art and life. It's thin and often we don't have to see it. It's okay to generally think of a singer as a singer and a movie star as a movie star. But they are not, those are archetypes consciously accepted by famous people. Inside of every artist, there is a person. And when we forget that, is when we trip on the line. It is almost cruelly funny that part of Close's work was revealing that person inside of his more famous subjects, a person who needs to be revealed. Because that is someone who can melt away, someone who can be eroded by years of positive reinforcement for the artist. When the person is gone, we are left with an artistic shell that does not know the line between art and life, someone who is unable to heed the lessons of their own work. Someone who is not revealed by paint or tile, but by brave women. This is a dilemma for every artist, and for every viewer of art. Mild versus harsh interruptions.

Citations

Cascone, Sarah. "See the Second Avenue Subway's Gorgeous New Art."
   Artnet News, Artnet News, 20 Dec. 2016, news.artnet.com/art-world/
   second-avenue-subway-art-unveiled-790343.

Kelly Prize for Excellence in First-Year Writing

Lunchtime Epiphanies
by Aditya Ravi
From COMPLIT 122: Engaged Writing
Nominated by Genta Nishku

Aditya's essay offers a reflection on the experience of being a second generation immigrant, taking elements of personal experience and using them to build original and refreshing analysis. Structured around the conventions of a narrative argument, this essay does an excellent job at combining analysis with story-telling. The narratives Aditya chose to write about center on intimate memories at the lunchroom and dining table, which then lead into an analysis that offers sharp and nuanced critical insights into identity and belonging.

Genta Nishku

Lunchtime Epiphanies

Lunchtime is a mysteriously powerful period. It's supposed to be a time for relaxation, a midday break from the stresses of modern life. For many like me, however, lunch brings uncertainty - it forces reflection on a search to find a cultural belonging in the world around me. As an Indian-American second-generation immigrant, lunch defines my life of inconsistency. Whether it's a PB&J sandwich or *keerai kutan* and *kathirikai curry*, my mid-day meal is in a constant state of flux, always shifting from one side to another. In the symbolism of lunch, I've found that my cultural identity elusively avoids fitting neatly into one box, the result of external forces in my daily environment. As second-generation immigrants, the attempt to fight back and establish a static cultural identity is impossible, and the only way to "find ourselves" is to allow these forces to continually mold us over time into diverse individuals. My lunchtime experiences offer a microcosm into this phenomenon and its effect on my own identity. The experiences may differ, but the struggle remains a pattern common amongst almost all second-generation immigrants - a static identity will never be found.

1.) <u>Pushed Away From Your Roots:</u>

I sat in the middle of the busy cafeteria, starving after a strenuous morning of macaroni art in my kindergarten class. All around me, children excitedly brought out their special lunch boxes with peanut butter and jelly sandwiches perfectly cut right down the diagonal. Others had a pre-packaged Snackable pack with ham, crackers, and most importantly, the coolest sticker prizes at the bottom - an extremely valuable trading commodity that made one the center of all attention. But I didn't need any of that, because I had the home-cooked meal that my mom, *Amma*, spent hours making from scratch the previous night. It didn't matter that I had no brightly-colored lunch box with stickers covering the sides, because all I needed was the taste of home. In that heat-preserving container I had a delicious meal of hand-rolled *roti* and piping hot *paneer makhani*, with a sizeable helping of steaming *basmati* rice and cool, refreshing *raita*. I pulled out my monochromatic tiffin carrier and began unscrewing the lid, my barrier to tasty nourishment. As soon as a small gap emerged between the carrier and its lid, my nose was met with a symphony of smell characteristic of *Amma's* cooking, smells that meant lunch and comfort every day for the first five years of my life.

But in that same moment, my ears were assaulted by a squeaky "EW! What *is* that?" from the esteemed "Snackable Boy" sitting across from me. Immediately, my lunch had stolen the attention away from his sticker collection, and I was met with a wave of disgust from the other peers with "normal lunches" sitting at my table, as they all - out loud - attempted to discern what "smelly goop" I had brought to the cafeteria. Under a barrage of demurral by my peers who all clearly voiced their negative opinions about the smell I had brought into the cafeteria, I shamefully closed up my tiffin carrier and left the delicious *roti* and *paneer* to waste, in the same way that *Amma* had carefully packed it that very morning. I'd committed a grave mistake by bringing in the food of my family's heritage into the cafeteria that day, for I'd yet to realize that the only accepted lunch meal was a peanut-butter jelly sandwich or a coveted Snackable pack that fit the mold of American culture - anything else was considered treasonous.

This is the first moment I realized that our world is not a laissez-faire environment: every day we struggle between forces that push and pull us into different molds of our cultural identity. With one comment from an innocent six-year-old who was simply trying to figure out why my lunch was different than his, I was unwillingly thrust into the complex sea of societal forces that constantly influence the way that we as humans react and believe in relation to others. At that moment, my innocent, protected childhood had been shattered by this inevitable discovery of such influences.

Ironic to its sense of personal ownership, an identity is never the result of its owner's creation. It is *always* the net impact of experiences that each individual goes through in his/her life. When I speak of identity, I don't speak of someone's beliefs or views on politics, religion, or philosophical debates. I speak of one's actions, how they are represented, and, most importantly, their identification to some culture, its languages, norms, and values. For a child not of Anglo-European descent, this means finding "one's sense of self as part of an ethnic group... choosing between American and [their own] cultures" (Torres 532). At birth, one has little external experience except in the sheltered environment of their family life, and their identity is the cultural product of their guardians. Granted, immigrant families are already shaped by a variety of cultural forces, but the children of these families are often raised in a protective bubble of one cultural ideology. As the offspring of immigrant parents, however, the moment we step out of the confines of our incubation, we are tossed around by the forces governing societal acceptance. This new exposure to forces is also a pattern that emerges among children of Anglo-European descent, but it rather presents them with a position of power, as their own "heritage" *is* the predominant culture, making it easy to find faults in other cultures - or other lunches. Because of this inherent power imbalance between children of Western and non-Western descent, nowhere is this change for second-generation immigrants more prevalent than in the elementary school cafeteria, as that is often the first time we are witness to several cultures. My pristine vision of cultural identity was immediately shattered the moment that I was brought out of the confines of a sheltered home environment, with just one disgusted sneer.

There comes a point in almost every immigrant child's life where they have to make a choice of culture, most often between their traditional heritage or the prevailing American cultural norm. Indiana University Professor of Education Vasti Torres communicates this obstacle in her academic discussion about the identity search of Latino/a immigrant students in an American setting: "The first stage [of a search for ethnic belonging] indicates a lack of probing into the concept of ethnicity.... Individuals in this stage tend to accept the values and attitudes of the majority culture" (533). It's a general pattern that children are pushed into adopting the predominant culture at first exposure. The second-generation immigrant child is not necessarily brought up with the knowledge or keen awareness that they are living in a world where multiple cultural influences will bombard them the second they step out of the confines of their incubation. When one meets the real world, it becomes easy to follow the tide and attempt to fit in to the prevailing American culture because it is the first time that their cultural identity has been subject to an opposing force. The school cafeteria is thus a black hole: it is witness to a multitude of different cultural backgrounds, which are all eventually sucked in to fit a prevailing societal ideal that strips individuals of their original cultural identity. In my experience, this pattern of adopting the prevailing culture is taken a step further, however, as the individual often concurrently *rejects* their ethnic cultural roots.

Overwhelmed with the dominant school lunch cultural force, I swiftly made the choice to forgo my own cultural roots and ride the wave of prevailing social norms, pleading *Amma* to make me peanut butter & jelly sandwiches instead of *dosa* or *idli* with *chutney*, yet she always refused to make me anything different. On a daily basis I would either bring back my tiffin-carrier exactly how it had been packed the same morning, or sneak a few small bites, carefully avoiding the watchful gaze of my peers and making sure to not let any of the "disgusting" smell creep into their noses. Time and time again I masked my heritage, and began to believe in the comments from my peers, that my food actually was gross. Through this, I developed a strong dislike of anything that associated me with the "smell" of my heritage, and ironically, I myself morphed into the same ignorant person who made fun of other lunches just because they didn't fit with the norm. I forced myself to fit the mold of the "normal" American child, to be on the other side of the power imbalance between cultures.

Like many second-generation immigrants, in the face of the first external influence from my environment, I wilted and forcefully rejected my cultural roots. Such patterns of shunning the abnormal are widely prevalent in the American cultural mixture from a young age, and are key pressures for children of non-European descent to alter their cultural identity. In fact, 43% of surveyed respondents in a study of Latin American students noted that negative experiences in college was at least a minor factor in their ethnic identity (Torres 537). Even in college, almost a majority of an immigrant demographic group felt that their negative environment pushed them towards some identity - the effect on a five-year-old who has not known anything but the culture of their own heritage would surely be much more drastic.

But these external influences are not just one-sided, as we have to deal with opposing forces that make cultural identification so much more difficult. As I grew up an American in an Indian body, I became somewhat of a stranger to the nurturing culture of my childhood, resulting in a new force on my identity, but this time from my Indian heritage, which threw me back into a state of complete confusion.

2.) <u>A Pull Back to Tradition:</u>

Soaking up the Sun in an idle, muggy morning in the depths of the dog days, I was thriving in the joys of summer vacation after fifth grade: no responsibilities, only sleep, play, and most importantly - lunch. Best of all, *Amma's* father, my *Thatha*, was flying in from India that morning to stay with our family for the duration of the summer, the first time he had come to the country in over ten years. The last time I'd seen him was when I was a toddler, so this would effectively be the first time that I met him, and I could not have been more excited.

All my life, everybody had told me how I emulated *Thatha* because we both enjoyed learning about nature and shared a profound love for music. According to *Amma*, he even had a collection of over 200 National Geographic Magazine issues, a goldmine of knowledge that I could tap into. To speak with *Thatha* would be to speak to the roots of my own personality - the genetic reason behind my interests. Every two minutes, I constantly ran up to *Amma* asking her how much longer it would take for *Thatha* to get home, because I wanted to be the first one to speak with the family member who was exactly like me.

That afternoon, I eagerly set the table for lunch, making sure to place my plate right next to where *Thatha* would sit, for I wanted to soak up all the knowledge he had brimming in his words. When he arrived, I would be able to speak with him and bond over a meal that *Amma* made special for the whole family. However, there was one problem: I couldn't speak *Tamil*, because I had refused to continue learning the language and could only understand certain phrases. Nonetheless, I made sure to refine the limited bank of phrases I knew, so I could chat in a patchwork *Tamil*-English hybrid. I had an endless list of questions to ask *Thatha*: How did he learn so much about nature? Where did he get all of his magazines? Did he play an instrument like I did?

Once *Thatha* arrived, our family sat down at the table for a fabulous lunch: steaming hot *vendakkai curry* delicately cut to ensure that the taste simmered down to the middle of each piece, *rasam* that cleared the sinuses with every sip, and sweet *manga kutan* to balance the spice of the other dishes. As we began to feast on the meal in front of us, I was getting ready to spew my barrage of questions - but I first needed some rice, some *chadam*, to start my meal.

Without hesitation, I casually asked *Thatha*, "Can you pass the rice, please?"

My words took a second to register in his mind, but served to impact him more than anything else I said that day. He scornfully glanced at me, then at *Amma*, and in *Tamil*, remarked, "Why doesn't Aditya speak in *Tamil*? What kind of Indian can't even speak his mother tongue?"

My world came crashing down in an instant: With one comment, *Thatha* had destroyed any hope I had that he would respect me for who I was, even though we were almost the same person. In that moment, I was thrown into a waterfall of guilt, wondering why I never held a closer tie to my Indian heritage, the culture and language of my entire family - was I not worthy of my own ethnicity? At the same time these thoughts raced around my head, *Amma* and *Thatha* were talking about how I never "appreciated" the value of my cultural heritage, which only served to worsen my confusion and guilt. But everything kept coming back to that one comment. *Thatha*, having lived his entire life essentially immersed in one Indian culture, was unfazed by my identification struggle and felt it blasphemous to even consider fitting into any other mold. In his words, I was essentially a traitor to my heritage, someone who didn't respect the toil of previous generations to give me the privileged life I had. I no longer had any sense of stability - only a serious lack of clear balance between my dual cultures. I had just discovered the true life of a second-generation immigrant.

This experience showed me the true issue that comes with living in America as a child of an immigrant family. In no other situation are environmental forces on one's identity so divisive and conflicting. Like many Asian-American second-generation immigrants in middle-class families, I have lived a privileged life that has been free of many obvious struggles, but the constant ebb and flow of trying to find a balance between cultures is one struggle that makes it impossible for me to forge a singular cultural identity. These forces do not discriminate with age or innocence - it is almost inevitable that one's perception of identity is shattered and pieced together multiple times, only to be broken again by an opposing force later in life. Torres labels this second common step in the lives of immigrant children as "Ethnic Identity Moratorium, which occurs when individuals are faced with a situation that forces them to initiate a [identity] search" (533). When my grandfather snapped at me just for using English, I realized how my attempt to force myself into the prevailing American culture had left me estranged from my Indian roots, which in turn threw me into a blind search to find a balance and a true cultural identity.

Considering this pattern, it can appear impossible to ever have a semblance of belonging to a specific community, for one is always acted on by an outside pressure. Too often we try to fight these forces, pushing back and convincing ourselves that we *belong* in one culture and not the other. Ironically, however, this push back against external forces is what often leads to the confusion of cultural belonging in the first place: in an attempt to mesh with the American cultural mold, I rejected all Indian food and language outside of my home. But the strength of cultural influences are inversely related to our affinity to them: as we distance ourselves further from our cultural roots, the pressure to "rejoin" the heritage only grows as older family and community members unable to understand our identity struggles impatiently drag us back to the traditional culture. In this way, my efforts to reject the influence of my Indian heritage only made it stronger, and my experience with *Thatha* sent me swirling back into a realm of confusion over my true cultural identity. The reality is that it is impossible to push ourselves to fit into *one* specific cultural mold, resulting in an uncomfortable state of constant change.

3.) <u>Finding a Sense of Belonging:</u>

Maybe an identity is found in this lack of comfort in identity. Effectively dealing with conflicting external forces on a cultural identity is logically the same as regaining control when a car begins to skid on ice: one must steer *into* the skid to find a sense of balance. When we allow experiences to fully shape who we are, we are not fighting back against the tide of forces influencing our identity: we are steering into the skid, diminishing conflict, and adapting to the changes without trying to completely assimilate into one specific cultural mold. I contend that the best solution to cultural misidentification amongst second-generation immigrants is best solved with admitting defeat: we will never have a static identity. This reality is confirmed by esteemed sociologist Stuart Hall, whose research shows that "identities emerge within the play of specific modalities of power, and thus are more the product of difference and exclusion, rather than a personal unity" (Gay and Hall 4). In other words, we are not in control of the identification we have with a cultural background, and the fabrication that identity is stagnant is incredibly misleading. Essentially, power imbalances between offsetting cultural forces push our identity one way or another, just as my "smelly lunch" experience in the cafeteria prompted me to force myself into a cultural mold. In turn my "identity" was washed away the instant the opposing influence of my own heritage became too powerful, and I myself realized that such attempts to establish a static identification are futile.

But one must note that a dynamic, constantly changing identity is not necessarily a bad thing. A main reason why so many second-generation immigrants are left with a feeling of helplessness in their search for identity is because they are obsessed with finding one cultural background to fit into. We are all subject to the influences of endless ideals that are thrown at us every day - when we fairly consider their value and accordingly allow them to influence us, then we are pushed towards a cultural identity that may not be the one of our conscious choosing, but is the best fit for us in the end. Confidently having a base in more than one culture allows one to broaden their own perspectives and establish their place in the societal fabric of their community. Allowing the opposing forces from environmental factors come to an equilibrium state through trial and error is thus how second-generation immigrants should find their balance between their heritage and the predominating culture.

I don't mean to say that a passive lifestyle is the ideal manner - we must be aware of our influences and whether they are beneficial to our development as active participants in our identity formation. The world is full of influential forces: some of them may harm our cultural identity with hateful messages, and others might help one develop as an individual. For instance, discriminatory beliefs - even as minor as the comments about my school lunch - may be influences on cultural values, but we must have the awareness to not allow those to shape who we are. In today's social-media driven climate, it is difficult to avoid exposure to forces that decrease our inter-cultural appreciation, but it is important to remain keenly aware of their effects. As individuals attempting to find one's self in the midst of a sea of potential identifications, it's important to value *how* influences might impact us before allowing the barrage of forces lead one to some cultural identity. When most second-generation immigrants float in the forces of their environment, they're able to land on a cultural balance that best fits individual needs. My cultural identity remains dynamic, but I'm now happy to live on the boundary between my Indian heritage and American home because it gives me access to varied perspectives (and foods), only because I have stopped fighting back against outside influences.

I'm in my dorm room, getting ready to scarf down some leftover *keerai kutan* my mom dropped off for me last weekend, and I am no longer scared to savor the taste of my heritage. My journey has seen a multitude of conflicting forces that have not allowed me to pick my own cultural identity throughout my childhood. From starting off in a sheltered environment, to rejecting my heritage, to falling into a haze of confusion about my cultural identification, I have followed the path of many second-generation immigrants. It is impossible to choose one's own identity because of the magnitude of forces that act on each child of immigrants, but trying to fight them will only result in further confusion; it is best to let the environment guide each of our proverbial search. I look at my Indian food on the plate in front of me, and know that the way that I see this culture will surely be different in a day, a month, or a year, because as the calendar flips pages, so will my identity. Lunchtime may remain a constant in our lives, but the experiences we gain within it will change us every day.

Works Cited

Hall, Stuart, and Paul Du Gay. *Questions of Cultural Identity*. SAGE Publications Ltd., 2012.

Torres, Vasti. "Influences on Ethnic Identity Development of Latino College Students in the First Two Years of College." *Project Muse*, John Hopkins University Press, 10 July 2003, muse.jhu.edu/article/44585/pdf.

Excellence in Multilingual Writing

Toyota Camry in China and the US: Same Name, Different Cars
by Xuanwen Huang
From Writing 120
Nominated by Scott Beal

Xuanwen's passion for automotive engineering shines through clearly in this essay in his careful research, knowledge of design features, and attention to detail. His essay argues that the demand for status and face-saving prestige in the Chinese market leads Toyota to emphasize "premium" features related to the car's appearance, while the US version of the Camry emphasizes practicality and fun in ways that may be less visible on the surface. The argument is both well-supported and well-organized, making his conclusions quite convincing.

Scott Beal

Toyota Camry in China and the United States: Same Name, Different Cars

The Toyota Camry is a well-recognized car model and one of the best-selling cars worldwide. I can see this car on the road all the time – both in China and in the United States. In fact, in the past month, October 2018, Toyota sold 26,914 units of Camry in the United States (Demandt), and the company sold 14,628 units of Camry in China ("Toyota Camry China Auto Sales Figures"). To achieve such impressive sales numbers in both countries, Toyota did not build their flagship model, Camry, in the same way. The company made several changes between two versions of the Camry in multiple areas, such as features, designs, engines, and even values that the car represents. This paper looks at and beyond two different advertisements of the Toyota Camry in China and the United States and focuses on the following question: what are the reasons for Toyota to make two different versions of the same model?

The advertisement for the United States version of Camry was played in Super Bowl 2015 (see fig.1).

Fig. 1. An Advertisement for Toyota Camry Played in Super Bowl 2015 from Wall Street Journal. "Super Bowl 2015: Toyota Camry Ad." *YouTube*, 26 Jan. 2015, www.youtube.com/watch?v=GNOzKxJTCoo. Accessed 21 Nov. 2018.

The advertisement was about pushing the limit – it featured a female who lost her legs and wearing artificial ones; however, unlike most people wearing limbs who walk relatively slow, she was doing activities which are hard and challenging for even non-disabled people. There was one scene that she was running with "blades" on a mountain, scenes of her practicing and performing ballet, one scene that she was modifying her limb in a shop, and scenes in which she fell when skiing but eventually mastered the skills. All these scenes showed her strong character and an attitude of never giving up. She drove her Camry to all those places, and the color of her car was red, very bright and noticeable color for any car. The ad ended with a picture of the red Camry with a description on top of the car, "THE BOLD NEW CAMRY" (Wall Street Journal). Overall, the advertisement indicated the Camry fits people who share a similar attitude to the female, bold and brave.

In comparison, the advertisement for the Camry in China had a very different style – most scenes in the 30-second ad were related to a white Camry rolling on the road (see fig.2).

Fig. 2. An Advertisement for the Chinese Version of Toyota Camry from "Fengtian Kaimeirui Xuanchuanpian [Toyota Camry Commercial]." *Iqiyi*, 22 June 2017, https://www.iqiyi.com/w_19rtrf6m7h.html. Accessed 21 Nov. 2018.

The beginning scene of the advertisement was shown in the screenshot, in which the Chinese version of Camry is entering a turn on a mountain. A spinning globe – only showing the equator and earth's axis – was added to the center of the turn by computer. There was a male's voice in the background, asking in Chinese, "是什么让它非比寻常地平衡" ("What makes it extraordinarily balanced"; "Fengtian Kaimeirui Xuanchuanpian [Toyota Camry Commercial]"). Then, the camera shifted to the inside of the car at the center console, showing a screen in the center and wood trim pieces on the side. The globe, on a smaller scale, was sitting at on the console and spinning smoothly. The voice in the background answered the previous question by himself, "是舒适, 是静谧, 是卓越品质" ("It's comfort, quiet, and outstanding quality"; "Fengtian Kaimeirui Xuanchuanpian [Toyota Camry Commercial]"). There were also scenes of the Camry on a cable-stayed bridge and at a house in the mountain. These locations were all tranquil that there were no vehicles and people other than the white Camry itself and the driver, who was only on screen for roughly a second, on display.

In the two advertisements, Toyota conveyed different messages to consumers in the United States and China. In the Superbowl ad for the Camry, the main message was the boldness of both the Camry itself and its owner. While the female in the ad was fighting against her destiny of being disabled, the United States version of Camry was like a loyal friend who was always with her. The car went through difficulties that happened to her and took her everywhere. Therefore, the Camry was essential to her – it was the Camry that helped her have such a bold character and a versatile life. In the advertisement for the Chinese version of Camry, however, the message was mostly based on the merits of the car, as the voice in the background suggested: quiet, comfortable, balanced, and good quality. Other than that, in the only scene of the driver, a male driving the Camry was mysteriously and confidently smiling. Considering all merits of the Camry listed in this advertisement, an implicit message here was the driver was smiling because of all those merits of the car.

In addition to the different messages behind the two advertisements, when putting the two advertisements together, they reveal how different the variations of the Camry could look. The most apparent difference between the two cars in the ad was the color. The United States version of the car featured a very special shade of red. The color fit the message behind the advertisement well that, similar to the woman, the vehicle was bold and active. The color choice in the Chinese version of the ad was much subtler. A pure white car on the mountain would make any person feel quiet and peaceful even without the message in the background describing how good the car was. Both colors fit into their respective theme well.

Taking a closer look to the car, the color was not the only difference between the two in appearance. The designs of the two variations were actually different. In the commercial for the United States, the red Camry in the commercial was curvier, as shown in the front grille and headlights; whereas, in the commercial played in China, the white Camry featured mostly straight lines in appearance. It is worth noting that the two cars were in the same generation. Both versions of the Camry were manufactured between 2015 and 2017, meaning they both belonged to the 7.5th generation of Toyota Camry in their respective market. Thus, the difference in design cannot be explained by different model years; it can only be concluded that their appearances were designed to be different.

According to Gratton, the different designs were part of Toyota's "regionalization strategy." These models, exported to China, are referred to as "prestige Camry" by Toyota (Gratton). As the name suggests, Toyota makes design changes to the car so that it could appear more prestigious. The way they achieve different looks can partially be seen from the two advertisements: less curvy but straighter lines and adding more chrome pieces to the exterior. Differences between the United States version and Asian version were most apparent during the lifespan of the 6th generation of Camry. The two variations of the car are shown in the figures below. The one in metallic silver is the United States version of the car (see fig.3).

Fig. 3. Image of the United States Version of the 6th Generation of Toyota Camry from "2007 Toyota Camry." *U.S. News & World Report*, https://cars.usnews.com/cars-trucks/toyota/camry/2007. Accessed 21 Nov. 2018.

It took a more radical design. The headlights were long, narrow, and shaped like a parallelogram-like a lot of cars in the current generation. For the Asian version of the car, the headlights were much thicker and square like. The front grille was also thicker, less inclined and decorated with chrome. On the side, the Asian version featured a rub rail with chrome to add layers to the car (see fig.4).

Fig. 4. Image of an Asian Version of the 6th Generation of Toyota Camry from "Toyota Camry (2007-2011)." TRAPO *Malaysia*, www.trapo.asia/my/car-mat/classic/camry-2007-2011-2/. Accessed 21 Nov. 2018.

These chrome pieces acted like accessories worn by people, making them look more elegant. This was the same case for the models in the ads, the Asian version featuring more chrome pieces and while the United States version being designed more active.

The two versions also varied in interior. I looked at the specification sheets for the current generation of Camry for both the Chinese market and for the United States market, and there were some significant differences. Firstly, I found that leather seats become standard for a Camry in China and the United States until the second lowest configuration and the highest configuration, respectively. Secondly, the interior of the Chinese version of Camry used wood-like trim pieces, while the United States version used metal-like trim pieces. Thirdly, based on what I saw, most of the United States version of Camry had black interior, as most of the Chinese variation combined black with beige: black on top of the central console and beige on the, mostly leather-made, seats.

But what were the reasons behind those changes? According to Paul Beranger, former Corporate Manager for Style and Design at Toyota Style

Australia, Toyota made those changes to "understand regional demands and meet regional expectations" (Gratton). In a lot of Asian countries including China, cars were given more meanings beyond its function of taking people from point A to point B: it becomes a representation of one's social prestige. Therefore, the "cultural demand" from people is a car that looks more premium. Psychologist Henri Tajfel's social identity theory can help understand this situation that the group people belonged to was an important source of pride and self-esteem (Morgan and Guthrie ch. 2). This theory was especially true to Chinese car customers because, a lot of times, Chinese customers are only allowed to have one vehicle due to the limitations for the number of licenses plates a family can own and the skyrocketing price for parking lots. Thus, the one and the only one car of a customer has become a direct representation of what group a person belongs to and how wealthy he, she, or their family was. This theory explained the format of the advertisement for the Chinese market very well. The ad listed so many merits of Camry, "comfort, quiet, and outstanding in quality," to prove one point: Toyota Camry is the car that you can drive to impress someone else and show your prestige.

Another theory was that consumers in China are driven by their "apprehension of losing face" (Liao and Wang 990), a concern that encompasses reputation from both individual and community perspectives. The term "face" is slang of how good one looks in Chinese. Since a car is relatively more expensive for an average person in China and makes an important part of how good a person looks, this "losing face" concern is a daily struggle for a lot of people. Therefore, a premium design and special features were implemented to provide the extra wealthy look for people.

This theory of worrying about losing face explained the differences in the interior of the two variations. Leather seats and wood trim pieces are features being considered as quintessential to add a car's luxury level, which is important for an individual's "face" in China as previously discussed. Therefore, car manufacturers try to add this feature to more trim levels to make the sale.

Color-wise, the Chinese version implemented a combination of black console, beige leather seats, and wood-like trim pieces to mimic the vibe inside of a luxury car. Whereas in the United States, since the car is much more practical and less representative, cloth seats in black color are preferred by a lot of customers that are cheaper, more stain-resistant, and do not become as heated/iced in hot/cold weather as leather seats do.

Since the Prestige Camry has so many more premium features than the United States version, you might be wondering whether the United States version is inferior to its Asian counterpart. The answer is not necessarily. Toyota tried every way to make the Prestige Camry looks better, but the most critical parts of a car are those that normally cannot be seen, and this is where the United States models are superior at. The engine capacities of the United States version of Camry are larger at 2.5L and 3.5L for the current generation; in comparison, engine capacities are 2.0L and 2.5L for Chinese models. Since the engine is under the hood, there is no way to be seen by other people. Therefore, it is irrelevant to the "losing face" issue. For customers in the United States, however, they are not buying a car to showcase in front of other people. The female in the ad, for example, she drove for her Camry to make her own life more versatile. Thus, the driving experience is much more important to customers in the United States – they need a car that can make themselves happy. Because of this, most car models in the United States feature at least one option for the engine that is high in capacity so that the model can still attract customers who need speed or fun. The Toyota Camry, although being considered as a family car, had no exception of providing a 3.5L option for customers.

In conclusion, different needs from customers decided how the model was "packaged" in the two countries. Toyota made two variations of their most classic model, Camry, to fit people's needs from two distinctively different cultures. Since the Camry adapted to each culture so well, there is no wonder that it becomes one of the best-sellers in both countries.

Works Cited

Demandt, Bart. "Toyota Camry US Car Sales Figures." *Carsalesbase.com*, carsalesbase.com/us-car-sales-data/toyota/toyota-camry/. Accessed 21 Nov. 2018.

"Fengtian Kaimeirui Xuanchuanpian [Toyota Camry Commercial]." *Iqiyi*, 22 June 2017, https://www.iqiyi.com/w_19rtrf6m7h.html. Accessed 21 Nov. 2018.

Gratton, Ken. "All Aboard the Aurion Express." *Carsales.com.au*, 22 Dec 2009, www.carsales.com.au/editorial/details/all-aboard-the-aurion-express-17789/. Accessed 21 Nov. 2018.

Gratton, Ken. "The Rise of TSA." Carsales.com.au, 10 Feb 2010, www.carsales.com.au/editorial/details/the-rise-of-tsa-18241/. Accessed 21 Nov. 2018.

Liao, J., and Lei Wang. "Face as a Mediator of the Relationship between Material Value and Brand Consciousness." *Chinese Journal of Physics*, vol. 47, no. 6, 2009.

Morgan, G. and Susan Guthrie. *Are We There Yet?: The Future of the Treaty of Waitangi*. Lower Hutt, The Public Interest Publishing Company Ltd, 2014.

"Toyota Camry China Auto Sales Figures." *Carsalesbase.com*, carsalesbase.com/china-car-sales-data/toyota/toyota-camry/. Accessed 21 Nov. 2018.

Excellence in Multilingual Writing

How Consuming Transgenic Food Would Affect Human Immune Systems?
by Zhiyao Zhang
From Writing 120
Nominated by Shuwen Li

Have you ever worried about consuming transgenic food? Do you know the differences between transgenic and genetically modified food? Relying on scientific evidence, Zhiyao (Bobby) addresses the public concern about transgenic food in his paper. Not only does Bobby translate the complex scientific knowledge surrounding transgenic food for lay consumers to clear their confusion, but also he demonstrates how such translation work can help build trust in the public.

Shuwen Li

How Consuming Transgenic Food Would Affect Human Immune Systems?

When we are shopping in the supermarkets, we often notice some foods, especially vegetables and crops that are labeled as non-transgenic. For the public, these non-transgenic labeled foods appear to be more appealing than those without the labels. Why does this happen? Some people would say the transgenic foods may harm their health. However, according to scientists, consuming transgenic foods benefits rather than harming our health. In this article, I aim to inform the public of the connection between consuming transgenic food and its effect on human health, in particular, our immune system. I also want to lead the public to think about the safety of consuming those transgenic foods and build people's trust in the foods.

Is Transgenic food equal to genetically modified (GMO) food?

Before talking about how consuming transgenic foods really affect our immune systems, we should first look at the public concern about these foods. The name "transgenic" is often confused with the word "genetically-modified" (GM). Indeed, GM means exactly what the words say: the genetic material is modified and therefore leads to natural or induced mutation. According to Dr. L. Curtis Hannah (2013), Professor of University of Florida, traditional GM investigators treat seeds with a powerful mutagenic agent and then screen progeny arising from these seeds for the trait of interest. The breeders also select against detrimental traits caused by the mutagen. These detrimental mutations are much more common than advantageous changes. These mutations sometimes cause unfavorable changes in some other traits and create problems in GM foods. On the other hand, transgenic foods, also known as bioengineered foods, are produced from organisms that have had changes introduced into their DNA, using the methods of genetic engineering. This process often introduces new traits as well as greater control over traits to the organisms that can benefit human consumptions.

For example, more than 90% of the corns in U.S are genetically modified in order to tolerate various herbicides and to express a protein that kills certain insects. Compared to GM foods that carry detrimental mutations, transgenic foods do not contain negative elements that may harm people's health based on recent scientific consensus. Yet, the public are much less likely to perceive transgenic foods as safe, particularly for their immune system. This concern is understandable because transgenic foods are modified in their DNAs, and the introduced DNA may attack our immune system like an foreign invading object.

Why focus on immune system?

The human immune system serves as a defense system for our body, which is crucial for living activities. It can detect and clean pathogens, referring to anything that can harm our body. The immune system itself can be divided into two major categories: congenitial immunity or non- specific immunity (you have this kind of immunity since you were born) and acquired immunity (you acquire this kind of immunity after some treatments) (Malcom, 2018, p. 575). Here I focused on the acquired immunity that can be improved by taking foods or vaccines. In contrast, the non-specific immunity cannot be influenced much by external interference. The disorder of immune system can cause many autoimmune diseases, inflammatory disease and most seriously—cancer (Brodin, 2017). However, people develop several ways to support our immune system. Consuming transgenically modified foods is one of the approaches.

Is having transgenic food safe?

Before we talk about how consuming transgenic foods can support our health, let's first clear some of the public concerns about the foods. The public are concerned mostly about whether the transgenic foods, especially the antibiotic marker genes, are safe for human health because when these genes express in plants, the antibiotic particles expressed in the plants may be transported to the human body and damage health (Aslam, 2011). To evaluate the damage, a research group from China conducted a study on transgenic apple fruits (Zhou, 2010). The researchers first extracted genes in apple fruits and transformed the extracted genes to E.coli so that the bacteria could express the genes and monitor the protein made from the genes. They used E.coli as the carrier of the genes because they had the similar gene expression pattern as humans and plants. The research group also introduced a positive control, indicating the upper limit of consumption of the expressed antibiotic marker gene and a negative control indicating the amount of this protein expressed in the normal nontransgenic fruit. If a person consumes more than that limit, the antibiotic will accumulate in his or her body and damage liver, kidney, or other organs. To test the amount of antibiotic protein, the researchers constructed a hybridization map to straightly visualize the amount. The result shows that the most of transgenic apples in this research can express this exogenous (not its own) gene but varies in the amount it expressed. The researchers interpreted that though different samples showed different npt II activity, because of the extracted and concentrated samples, the results showed that no sample exceeded the upper limit positive control (Zhou, 2010, p. 3). Therefore, although the antibiotic proteins could be expressed in those transgenic fruits, it does no harm to our body because the amount of those proteins is low. Based on the above research results, we can conclude that it is safe to eat antibiotically modified foods.

How transgenic animal products benefit our immune systems?

Not only is it safe to consume transgenic foods, but also it is beneficial. Some kinds of animal products can be modified to express a certain type of protein in it in order to provide antibiotic supplement to human body. Cooper and Caitlin (2013), a group of researchers from University of California, focused on the transgenic goat milk, which can also be served as an alternative for normal milk with a simpler modification in the genes. One study done by this group revealed how consuming transgenic milk can help resolve diarrhea, a common kind of disease in children of developing countries. Those researchers transgenitically modified the goat milk to express the protein of human lysosome, a protein which is only expressed in mammalian milk but not in ruminant milk like goat or cow milk used, to target many kinds of bacteria. Once the signs of infection were discovered in those pigs, pigs were fed with hLZ (human lysozyme)-milk or non-transgenic control goat milk three times a day for two days. They used both the technique of clinical observation and complete blood content to qualitatively and quantitatively measure the result of the bacteria activity and the dehydration level of the pigs, where dehydration is a common symptom of diarrhea. The result turned out that a significant drop in the diarrhea symptom took place and pigs that consumed transgenic goat milk had a much quicker recovery from the disease. The research group suggested that this kind of transgenic milk can help defend the possible diarrhea caused by E.coli, which provides solution to children diarrhea for mothers suffering from the absence of lysosome in their milk.

Moreover, this group of researchers found that when young pigs consumed this kind of transgenic milk, they would express more cytokine TGF-beta1, a crucial anti-inflammatory factor in all mammals that is induced by the protein lysosome (Cooper, 2011, p.1237). They hypothesized that consuming this transgenic milk with lysosomes can potentially impact intestinal health positively. The method they used was almost the same as the research done above but the data interpretation is different. They performed the quantitative real-time PCR to assess local expression of anti-inflammatory factors in the small intestine to show how much of these factors were induced by lysosomes. The data showed that a significant increase was observed in three factors in the ileum of the pigs where they took the sample from, along with an increase in intraepithelial lymphocytes. These data showed that consuming the transgenic milk containing hLZ prevents inducing an inflammatory response, and moreover improves the health of the small intestine in pigs (Cooper, 2011, p.1243). Therefore, this kind of milk is potentially helpful for humans and can support the immune system.

Some people would argue that because all these experiments are performed on animals, are these results applicable to humans? To answer this question, we need to consider the safety and ethical problems—all these studies cannot be performed on human bodies directly. Researchers must first perform experiments on animals or model organisms. For example, all experiments mentioned in the previous studies were taken place on pigs or mice. However, the results are still convincing because all mammals share a common immunization mechanism.

How can transgenic plants improve our immune system?

Transgenically modified crops or plants can express or enhance the concentration of some daily essential nutrients, which include various kinds of vitamins and phytonutrients like polyunsaturated fatty acids. Cathie Martin and Jie Li (2017) found that both of these transformations in crops are common and effective, and among those examples of the transformations, the biofortification (the idea of breeding crops to increase their nutritional value) of vitamin A is a great example to illustrate this idea (p. 699). Vitamin A is a group of unsaturated nutritional organic compounds that are crucial for growth and for sight development as well as the body health maintenance and immune support. Deficiency of Vitamin A can cause potential damage to retina, which may eventually lead to blindness if the deficiency is serious. However, this serious problem cannot be solved easily. According to UNICEF, Vitamin A deficiency is estimated to affect approximately one third of children under the age of five around the world, especially in those developing countries. The solution to this problem which came to scientists' mind is that they can modify crops to express vitamin A, acting as a supplement to normal meals. Rice is a suitable carrier for vitamin A because more than 70% population in the world consumes rice every day and the convenience to process rice from crop enables rice to keep vitamin A from degradation. In order to express vitamin A in rice, scientists transfer the gene segments that bacteria use to encode Vitamin A to the seeds, and the crop then can have the rice with Vitamin A expressed (Martin, 2017, p. 701). The first generation of Golden Rice can express 1.6μg/g vitamin A. Comparing with the suggested intake of vitamin A for children under 8 is 400μg per day, if a child has

250g of golden rice a day, the child can meet the daily requirement. Moreover, later generations of Golden Rice have improved greatly in the concentration of vitamin A for more than 7μg/g, suggesting that this kind of transgenic food can really provide sufficient supplementary nutrients to the human body (Martin, 2017, p. 701).

Another application for transgenic plant is to produce oral vaccine from them, which is a more economical and more convenient way of producing vaccine. Unlike the normal vaccine production that requires animal embryos (e.g., eggs), plant oral vaccine only requires transgenic plants to express antibodies. Then antibodies can be extracted to make pills for people to take. The process costs less and enables the mass production of the vaccines, ignoring the limit and cost of animal embryo. As early as 1995, Hugh Mason and Charles Arntzen (1995) predicted that because plants can produce vaccine antigens in a native and immunogenic way, the "bio-pharming" of vaccines is possible. If the antigens are orally active, food-based vaccines could allow economical production and delivery in developing countries (p. 388). Their prediction initiated a new aspect in vaccine research. Adopting the idea, the research done by Ghiasi, Salmanian, Chinikar, and Zakeri (2011) presented strong evidence. The research group fed mice with the oral vaccine produced from root and leaf of the transgenic tobacco plant which produce CCHFV glycoprotein. This protein stimulated the production of immunoglobin-G (IgG), an antibody in human body that targeted the Crimean-Congo hemorrhagic fever, a severe kind of fever only found in human but not animals whose death rate is more than 20% after infection. Their result indicates that the mice fed with the transgenic plant vaccine show a significant rise in specific IgG antibodies, suggesting that oral immunization of animals with products from transgenic plants is feasible and therefore can be an economical, sufficient substitute of the conventional production of vaccine.

Conclusion

As we can see, it is scientifically verified that consuming transgenic food and transgenic products does not harm our health; rather, it improves health and provides supplement nutrition. However, scientifically verified conclusion may not be sufficient to remove the fear of the public. In order to resolve public fear of transgenic food, scientists and governments need to spell out the values and assumptions behind risk assessment (Martinelli, 2013). For example, scientists and government could make animations to illustrate the science behind transgenic foods and use social media to circulate the knowledge among the public. When the public understand more about the nature of transgenic foods, they will be able to make more informed decisions, which will eventually motivate scientists to advance their studies on the transgenic foods.

References

Andreasen, M. (2014). GM food in the public mind–facts are not what they used to be. *Nature biotechnology, 32*(1), 25.

Aslam, W, A, M & Saeed, A. (2015, March 29). Risks and concerns of transgenic food. *Technology times, 6*(12), 27.

Brodin, P., & Davis, M. M. (2017). Human immune system variation. *Nature reviews immunology, 17*(1), 21.

Cooper, C. A., Brundige, D. R., Reh, W. A., Maga, E. A., & Murray, J. D. (2011). Lysozyme transgenic goats' milk positively impacts intestinal cytokine expression and morphology. *Transgenic research*, 20(6), 1235-1243.

Cooper, C. A., Klobas, L. C. G., Maga, E. A., & Murray, J. D. (2013). Consuming transgenic goats' milk containing the antimicrobial protein lysozyme helps resolve diarrhea in young pigs. *PloS one, 8*(3). doi:10.1371/journal. pone.0058409

Ghiasi, S. M., Salmanian, A. H., Chinikar, S., & Zakeri, S. (2011). Mice orally immunized by a transgenic plant expressing the glycoprotein of Crimean-Congo hemorrhagic fever virus. *Clinical and Vaccine Immunology, 18*(12), 2031-2037. doi:10.1128/CVI.05352-11

Hannah, Curtis. (2013, June 20th). What's difference between transgenic and genetically modified? Message posted to https://gmoanswers.com/ask/whats-difference-betweentransgenic-and-genetically-modified

Malcolm, H& Malcolm, S. (2018). The immune system. *Anaesthesia & Intensive Care Medicine, 19*(10), 575-578.

Martin, K & Li, J. (2017). Medicine is not health care, food is health care: Plant metabolic engineering, diet and human health. *New Phytologist, 216*(3), 699-719. doi: 10.1111/nph.14730

Martinelli, L., Karbarz, M., & Siipi, H. (2013). Science, safety, and trust: the case of transgenic food. *Croatian medical journal, 54*(1), 91. doi: 10.3325/cmj.2013.54.91

Mason, H. S., & Arntzen, C. J. (1995). Transgenic plants as vaccine production systems. *Trends in biotechnology, 13*(9), 388-392.

Zhou, R. J., Fang, Q., Shi, X. X., & Du, G. Q. (2010). Detection of npt II Activity in Transgenic Apple Fruits. Proceeding from iCBBE 2010: 4th International Conference on Bioinformatics and Biomedical Engineering. Chengdu, China. 1-3. IEEE.

Excellence in the Practice of Writing

How to Succeed in Writing 100 Without Really Trying (Disclaimer: You Should Actually Try)
by Michelle Karls
From Writing 100: The Practice of Writing
Nominated by Stephanie Moody

Through an interactive board game, Michelle Karls encourages future Writing 100 students to reflect on their own writing practices and develop tools for successfully navigating their first-year writing courses. The object of the game is to finish all final drafts completely while navigating common writerly issues like writer's block and procrastination. The game also draws from Michelle's first assignment of the semester, a writing narrative in which she reflected on her writing process and identity as a writer, to offer advice and strategy cards that can assist players as they move through the game. Michelle's humor, work ethic, and relatable writing struggles shape the board game experience and offer a perspective of the writing process that is both accessible and engaging.

Stephanie Moody

How to Succeed in Writing 100 Without Really Trying (Disclaimer: You Should Actually Try)

For this Remediation project, I aimed to design and create a board game that would give general writing advice as well as Writing 100 specific advice to anyone that played it. My goal was to engage the audience through the game, as opposed to having them just read an essay. The original goal of the Writing Narrative project focused on helping me to become a stronger writer by looking at how I wrote essays. I went into great detail about my procrastination habits, and explained how I wanted to try and change those habits so that I wouldn't write my papers the night before their due date. In this Remediation project, I aimed to get the players thinking about their writing processes, specifically their procrastination habits, if they had any. By playing the game, players can realize the detrimental effects of procrastination in an entertaining yet educational setting. When choosing a board game as a medium, I did not need to take into consideration the affordances and constraints a board game would provide, as I have made board games for classes before. I experienced their versatility, both in the ease of designing and the efficiency they provide in conveying information through game pieces and instruction manuals. Board games are very engaging, and I wanted to make future Writing 100 students think about their writing processes before they need to think about utilizing it fully for the first or second time since high school.

While essays are a formal style of writing and information communication, board games provide that information in an entertaining way. When writing the Writing Narrative essay, I utilized more formal and serious diction, as opposed to less formal diction in my board game manual and playing cards. Readers that read informal writing feel more invited into the piece of writing they are reading, an aspect of informal writing which my board game exploits. This modification covers the shift from informative writing that is only interesting to a select group of people, like my Writing Narrative essay, to instructive writing present in the game instructions that is interesting for a constantly changing audience. Because of the constantly changing audience, I added writing advice, as the game is meant specifically for Writing 100 students. I had no need to give writing advice at the beginning of the semester because I knew just as much or less about good writing as the audience for which my essay was intended, whether the audience was my peers in peer review or my professor.

One rhetorical choice that I made in the Narrative project that I did not alter in the Remediation project was the funny and entertaining tone I utilized. While the diction itself was not humorous, the overall content of both pieces was intended to make the audience laugh. The purpose of the humor, however, varied slightly. In the Narrative project, I included humor because I am a naturally funny person, but also because I know that reading essays is boring. In the Remediation project, the humor is meant to keep the players engaged by laughing amongst themselves and relating to the funny distractions on the procrastination cards together, because a large part of Writing 100 that helped me was developing relationships with the people in the class outside of just reading their rough drafts.

As I revised the Narrative project, my main takeaway was that what works for me in terms of writing may not and will not work for everyone else. For example, the time crunch that inevitably comes with procrastination is often my main source of motivation, but for others it can be restrictive and incite panic, not productivity. Additionally, I learned that writing is different for everyone, whether because of their personal writing backgrounds or interests, but that the same general guidelines apply to every academic piece of writing. For example, procrastination-induced stress should not be the main driving force behind a writer writing his paper.

The most important change in perception that I had when revising was in regards to my own writing process. In my first writer's memo, I stated that I wanted to procrastinate less, because I knew that college would be more stressful than high school and I would not be able to feasibly procrastinate as much as I would like. Looking back now, I realize that I changed almost nothing about my writing process, yet I believe that people should change their writing processes on the chance that it will benefit their writing. I sincerely hope that my board game would be a helpful tool in helping others to succeed in this wonderful class.

How to Succeed in Writing 100 Without Really Trying
Disclaimer: You Should Actually Try

<u>Summary:</u> Be the first person to complete the semester of Writing 100 with the highest grades! Move forwards (and occasionally backwards) on the calendar spaces until you have received a grade for each major project. The player with the highest grades (most points) at the end of the semester wins.

<u>How to Play:</u> Each player takes a turn rolling a die and moving the correct number of spaces. Depending on what space they land on (see <u>Spaces</u> below), they will complete a certain action. Their turn is over once their action is completed, then the turn progression continues to the next player.

<u>How to Win:</u> The player with the most points at the end of the game wins. Earn points by reaching the four final project deadlines and receiving a letter grade for each. Letter grades are determined by the order players reach each deadline space. The first person to reach each final space receives an A (4 points), the second a B (3 points), the third a C (2 points), and the fourth a D (1 point). The only exception is with the fourth final draft; when a player receives an A for the fourth final draft, they receive 5 points instead of 4. Letter grades B, C, and D keep their original points. Additionally, the first person to reach each rough draft space receives 1 point. Everybody after the first person receives no points from a rough draft. If, due to a procrastination card, a player gets sent back over a rough draft or final draft space, they do not lose their points or, if applicable, their letter grade.

<u>Spaces:</u> There are 7 types of spaces:

Rough Draft (orange)- These spaces are the rough draft due dates. Players automatically stop on this space.

Final Draft (red)- These spaces are the final draft due dates. Players automatically stop on this space.

Writer's Block (black)- Players that land on these spaces get sent to the Writer's Block, a separate space outside the calendar board. On their next turn, they must roll a die to get out. If the die shows a 5 or higher, they get out of jail. If a player rolls too low, they stay in jail and roll again on their next turn. They must roll a 3 or higher on their second turn, and if they still do not roll high enough, they automatically get out on their third turn. Once a player is out of the Writer's Block, they start their next turn at the last blank space they passed. If, on their next turn, they land on another Writer's Block space, players automatically move one space forward and treat the next space as a blank space.

Writing 100 Advice (green)- When a player lands on this space, they draw a green card and read the advice out loud. The card is then placed in a discard pile. Once there are no more green cards, green spaces turn into blank spaces. This mimics the flow of the class, where most of the writing advice for the class is giving at the beginning of the semester.

Procrastination (yellow)- When a player lands on this space, they draw a yellow card and read it out loud. Then, they are subject to the consequences of that card and must do what it says. The card is then placed into a discard pile. Once there are no yellow cards remaining, the discard pile gets shuffled and put back into play, to mimic the never-ending process of procrastination and distraction.

Good Practices (purple)- Similar to the Writing 100 Advice cards, Good Practices cards detail good things to do when writing. However, these cards are more general and read like accomplishments. Players that land on this space draw a purple card and read it out loud. These are positive cards that are meant to reinforce good writing practices. Like the Procrastination cards, Good Practices cards are shuffled and put back into play to reinforce good writing habits.

Blank Spaces (white and blue)- Blank spaces are blank spaces. Nothing happens when a player lands on a blank space. Special blank spaces include Fall Break and Thanksgiving Break, which are denoted in pink.

Cards:

The cards players draw are the same colors as the spaces players land on. Listed below are examples from each type of card.

Writing 100 Advice- Start early! Don't wait until the night or two nights before a due date to start writing. Your work will suffer because of it and you will be more crunched for time than you might think.

Procrastination- MoJo just put out a fresh tray of cookies. Lose a turn.

Good Practices- Make an outline! They guide your writing and keep it focused.

Note: It is possible to move zero or negative spaces depending on the procrastination card a player picks up.

Game Board Design: See image below.

Excellence in the Practice of Writing

Who I Am and Who I Want to Be Cannot Connect
by Anonymous
From Writing 100: The Practice of Writing
Nominated by Gina Brandolino

For this assignment, students were asked to take one of their previously written papers for the course (all text-based formal analyses) and revise it to make it a personal essay for an audience of their choice. Up to this point, students had not written about their personal experiences or feelings about our course topic, which was monsters. This assignment asked them to connect meaningfully with that course topic—and to address a new audience. For all other papers, papers were addressed to the audience of our class. Students were asked to envision a totally different audience.

This student's essay is amazing, a tour de force. He dives deep into the uncomfortable realities of not feeling at home in his home, with his family, and the price he pays for being different in ways he cannot and should not have to control. He builds bridges between our course readings and his own experiences that allow readers to better understand each. Most impressively, though, his essay is a series of steps out of the darkness and into the light where he claims his identity and stands up not just for himself but for others who are different in ways similar to and dissimilar from him.

Gina Brandolino

Who I Am and Who I Want to be Cannot Connect

Dear Papa,

Ever since I was eight years old, I told you that I want to be a dentist. The idea was built on my odd enjoyment of going to the dentist. I felt comfortable in the dental chair and loved how it felt to have dental work done. I think the premise developed because we were always personally close to our dentists. I grew fond their personalities and dreamed of living the lifestyle they had. When I was 11, I got braces and my visits to the dental clinic became more frequent, increasing from once every six months to once a month. In the two and a half years I had braces, my strong interest in the dental clinic changed. My attention focused more on individual orthodontists and dentists, and less on the aesthetic of the dental offices or the enjoyment of being worked on. I began finding the man behind the mask to be attractive. His large, muscular hands handled the tools with a pleasing force. His tight, beige dress pants defined the area around his groin. I loved the way his voiced mesmerized me when he would ask to "open wide" or "close my mouth." After a handful of years later and a couple more unique encounters, I came to the long-awaited conclusion that I was gay. The idea had never crossed my mind until my 17th birthday and I was proud of it, but the in following week, my thoughts began to change.

We went out for dinner with Mama at P.F. Chang's for your 64th birthday. After being seated, the flamboyantly dressed, young, male waiter came to take our orders. Although I do not know for certain whether or not he was gay, his appearance resembled the widely perceived stereotype of gay males and that was enough for you. You commented on his walk, the way he dressed, the odd tone in his voice, and other arbitrary physical attributes. I was so confused, thinking how you could make such crude judgements and be so disgusted. The worst part was that you told me to never be that way. Never to be somebody who dressed in bright clothes or dyed their hair blonde. You took your hurtful comments and slight anger and projected them on me as if I was the cause of your discomfort and disbelief. I told you "I understand" but the real me really did not understand. How could you be so insensitive? I want to offer you my perspective: a set of encounters that I have experienced over the past two years with textual support from readings in my English class. I believe that if you can consider my viewpoint, it can help you to be more open-minded and more accepting of individuals regardless of whether or not you agree with it.

In class, we read "Just Walk On By" by Brent Staples; The author focuses on how the society he lives in views him as dangerous purely off of his identities. Moreover, Staples centers one of his claims on his fear of law enforcement, and the increased potential of being arrested. He emphasizes that there is a distressing relationship between the two parties. For example, he begins to change his behavior to appear less threatening to others and he begins to implement strategies in his everyday life to assist with this. Towards the end of the essay, Staples writes, "I began to take precautions to make myself less threatening. I move about with care, particularly late at night … I whistle melodies from Beethoven and Vivaldi and the more popular classical composers" (Staples, 189). It is not common for individuals to whistle classical melodies while walking down the street, and the behavior comes off as odd. Staples is clearly afraid of the giving the wrong impression because he resorts to extreme and abnormal behaviors to protect himself. In a similar sense, I hold the same fear as Staples. Our relationship is often distressing, and I find myself resorting to unusual behaviors. Moreover, I am genuinely afraid of what would happen if I was honest.

In the summer of 2017, when we went to Armenia to visit family, I was not careful enough in hiding who I was. We went to downtown Yerevan and walked around late at night with a couple of your cousins. We eventually settled down at a local café and order some salted peanuts. You were engaged in a conversation with the cousins who only spoke Armenian. Because I do not know Armenian, I could not be a part of conversation. I ended up passing the time by fooling around on my phone. At the time I had been talking to a guy I met online. I sent Dylan a text and waited for his reply. You abruptly turned to me and snatched my phone out of my hand to see what I was doing. I tried explaining that I was just talking to a friend back home, and that it was nothing to worry about, but you did not buy into it. After briefly reading a couple messages, you realized I was not talking to friend home but rather a stranger. Thankfully, you did not investigate the situation further because we were out in public, but you had instructed me to block his number. Ever since the night in Yerevan, I have taken more cautious approaches to avoid being exposed. For instance, I deliberately have worked as many closing shifts at work as possible to avoid running into you at home. It is unsettling yet fulfilling to know that I have found ways around seeing you.

Staples also believes that changing his appearance will help society to not view him as a monster. For instance, Staples describes the clothes he wears and states, "Virtually everybody seems to sense that a mugger wouldn't be warbling bright, sunny selections from Vivaldi's *Four Seasons*" (Staples, 189). As denoted by the author, Staples purposely dresses in oddly bright clothes to appear less harmful. He does this because the society he lives in equates bright clothes with nonharmful individuals. His behavior of dressing in bright clothing and whistling classical melodies are examples of how the law enforcement officers have control over Staples. The author should not have to purposely dress a particular way or change his behavior for the purpose of appearing less harmful. The law enforcement officers indirectly have control over what Staples does because Staples alters his behavior and wardrobe to satisfy them. In a similar sense, I feel as if you have control over me and how I present myself. I intentionally purchase clothes I think would think you would like and often wear your old coats with the intent that you would be satisfied with who I was. Furthermore, I faked my enjoyment when we went to trains shows and events, but eventually I forced myself to find enjoyment in the same things you liked. I created this idea that it was wrong to like something that you did not like and vice versa. In retrospect, you indirectly controlled what I found enjoyment in and prevented me from exploring my own interest. As a consequence, I was heavily dependent on you and never learned to be independent.

By understanding the idea of social and cultural difference in the essay by Staples, we can understand Staples's point of view from a new perspective. As a general definition, someone who is seen as socially and culturally different is defined as someone who does not hold the same qualities as the majority of individuals in the society. They are also viewed as abnormal by the people within the norm. Staples' difference in the society he lives in stems from his physical appearance and how others view him as dangerous. For example, Staples discusses a time when he was browsing through stores and writes, "I entered a jewelry store … The proprietor excused herself and returned with an enormous red Doberman pinscher straining at the end of a leash. She stood, the dog extended toward me, silent to my questions, her eyes bulging nearly out of her head" (Staples, 188). Without having done anything, the proprietor feared Staples. She merely saw his appearance and decided that it was necessary to bring out a guard dog for security purposes. Staples's appearance is not the only factor that others depict him as dangerous to the society around him. His threating character derives from the idea that he deviates from the norm. He is seen as abnormal and people of the culture his lives in fear abnormality. Synonymous to the proprietor, I have seen you quickly evaluate others based on their appearances and classify them by stereotypes. By this way of thinking, you think almost everyone you see is in some way abnormal. For instance, I notice the strange comments you make about individuals when you drive. The family got ready one mid-summer Sunday morning and headed to church. We were turning into the parking lot when someone abruptly pulled out of a parking spot and almost hit your new 2018 Jeep Grand Cherokee. You were easily frustrated and said, "he should be shot." I understood your slight irritability but did not understand why or how you could say something so extreme. It has been many small encounters like this where you take it to the extreme and it is not necessary. The slightly abnormalities and inconsistencies make you uneasy.

The idea of social and cultural difference is also represented in the story by Karen Russell. In class, we read "St. Lucy's Home for Girls Raised by Wolves" which follows a group of girls with wolf characteristics as they go through a school that teaches them human characteristics and behaviors. More specifically, it focuses on one girl and her abstract thoughts about the culture and the people around her that make up the society she lives in. Furthermore, they were raised by wolves and they exemplify an entirely different culture than their human society. Russell writes about the nuns and states, "The nuns, they said, would make us naturalized citizens of human society. We would go to St. Lucy's to study a better culture" (Russell, 326). The girls would not be able to be a part of the human society based on their original cultural context. Their differences from the human society norm separates them so much that they have to go to St. Lucy's to receive special education to fit in with the norm. St. Lucy's Home, in essence, is culturally assimilating the girls to behave in a particular way that is considered normal by the people of the human society. Similarly, I often feel alienated from the world around me. Growing up, you heavily stressed Armenian culture and traditions in the household. Thus, I was not exposed to American culture likes my peers were. I noticed these differences developing in middle and high school when my friends would talk about movies, songs, or with slang. I could not engage with them because I did not understand what they were talking about. Eventually, I learned to accept that I would always be a little behind and that I would have to put more effort in than the people around. Although failing to socialize with my peers is not the most critical component in this letter, I want to mention it because I feel that it has value. For instance, I believe that opening yourself up to other cultures, especially American culture and philosophies, can help you be a more understanding individual in society and the exposure itself is beneficial in a social context.

On the other hand, Staples experiences a similar disconnect from his culture and the society he lives in. For instance, Staples is viewed as different because of his physical appearance. He recently moved to "a relatively affluent neighborhood in an otherwise mean, impoverished section of Chicago … It also made it clear that I was indistinguishable from the muggers who occasionally seeped into the area from the surrounding ghetto" (Staples, 186). Staples was living in an environment where the majority of individuals were not African American. The neighborhood that he was living in was not used to seeing Staples on a regular basis and began to view him as socially and culturally different. While comparing the story by Russell and the essay by Staples, it is not only illustrated that being culturally and socially different is viewed as erroneous, but the girls and Staples are considered to be abnormal and even monstrous in some cases. Like Staples and the girls, I feel disconnected. Particularly, I feel disconnected from home life. Back in high school, you would ask me to sit on the couch with you and watch television. You liked the history channel and especially the show *Ancient Aliens*. I would always say that I had studying to do and could not afford to spend time with you even when I did not have work to do. The real reason is that I did not want to sit next you. The idea made me uncomfortable and I loathed it. I would go up to my room and close myself off in solitude. I hated how I found as many excuses as possible to avoid being around you. I also hated how I felt better knowing that I was not with you. Eventually, the atmosphere of home life faded. I spent so much time avoiding you between school, work, and sitting in my room alone that being home began to feel artificial.

In both the story and the essay, there exists a relationship in which one party is superior to the other party. In this relationship, the superior person or group has control over the inferior person or group. Furthermore, it means that the inferior party changes their behavior to satisfy the needs of the superior party and prevent possible suppression. In Russell's story, the nuns are superior to the girls. For example, the nuns give each of the girls a human name when they first arrive. The nuns were forceful in their actions and chased Mirabella for "two hours to pin her down and tag her" (Russell, 327). Mirabella saw the nuns give the other girls a human name and she decided that she did not want to receive one. The nuns displayed their superiority to the girls by utilizing their power. They ultimately gained control and dominance in the situation, despite Mirabella's attempt at avoiding them. Under the control of the nuns, her idea of escape is irrational. On the other hand, law enforcement officers are cut out to be superior to Staples in the essay. For instance, Brent Staples describes a time when law enforcement officers mistook him for someone who he is not, and he writes "… I was mistaken for a burglar. The office manager called security and, with an ad hoc posse, pursued me through the labyrinthine halls, nearly to my editor's door. I had no way of proving who I was. I could only move briskly toward the company of someone who knew me" (Staples, 188). The law enforcement officer generalized Staples based off his looks and assumed that because he was running, that he was most likely fleeing a scene. The officer went to extreme measures by following Staples intensely through the complex building. The story and the essay are similar when comparing these two examples because they both demonstrate an instance in which the dominating figure intensely pursues the inferior figure. Mirabella fears the nuns while Staples fears the law enforcement officer. By looking at the unhealthy relationships in both of the stories, the "superior" one can control the "inferior" one by initiating a sense of fear.

Likewise, I hold fears just like the girls and Staples. I have feared what would happen if I was honest with you because I know how much it would change our relationship. I have falsified so much about myself when I am around you and presented only the characteristics that you would like. As a kid, I remember when you would take me to the Michigan football games in the fall before we moved to Illinois. You enjoyed the games so much, but I could not. I tried to find some aspect whether it was the energy of the crowd or overpriced meals at the concession stand. I expressed my marginal interest in attending the games, and it made you unhappy. I realized that it would be easier to lie about the enjoyment I had to keep you satisfied. I slowly began applying this concept to other parts of life and created a pseudo-version of myself. I had kept up the persona because I know it would be a lot for you to hear everything I had bottled up inside.

Despite your strong close-minded opinions, this letter would be incomplete if I didn't acknowledge the various positive things you have done for me and for the community. During school, you pushed me to do my best and continually challenged me to achieve more and more. When I met one expectation, you came back and told me to achieve a higher one. It made secondary school difficult and long, but I am glad you did it. You taught me to have a strong work ethic and always strive to be the best. Furthermore, you brought me to church every Sunday where I was able to learn about our faith and religion. Sunday School taught me the history, culture, and traditions of the Armenian people. You also enlisted me in Boy Scouts and I was the most reluctant to participate in the early years. You kept me in the program, and I am glad that you did because I soon came to realize that the program could teach me useful skills. For instance, I saw improvement in my organizational, planning, and critical thinking skills as a result of the program. In addition, you have done so many great things for the community we live in. For example, you volunteer at almost every fundraiser at church, and participate as an active leader on the Parish Council. It would be wrong to not acknowledge the many wonderful things you have done for me and for the community.

Just like the girls from St. Lucy's and Staples, the gay waiter is human with characteristics that make him a unique individual. Uniqueness and individually provides for a diverse environment, However, your verbal thoughts and actions create a stressful and unsettling environment. The society Staples lives in uses his characteristics and traits against him in a negative manner. His features present him as more suspicious, grabbing additional attention from others who are not like him. He is uncomfortable knowing that he has to change so other people and society will not misperceive him. My experience of living in the closet is difficult and uncomfortable. Conforming to your standards over time to satisfy you has developed a relationship that I am not content with. I want to change my bad habits of avoiding you in my room and rather spend time with you. I want to change my work schedule, so I can see you more often, but I am afraid. I am afraid that your closed-minded viewpoint will not accept who I am. I am wary knowing that being honest might worsen our relationship. I write this letter with the intent to come out and be honest in hopes that you can be honest with me. I hope we can come to an understanding.

CPSIA information can be obtained
at www.ICGtesting.com
Printed in the USA
LVHW030434150519
617863LV00011B/131